HAMPSTI
HIGHGATE
IN
50
BUILDINGS

LUCY McMURDO

AMBERLEY

For Mac, Jo, Ben and Emily – my wonderfully supportive family

First published 2022

Amberley Publishing, The Hill, Stroud
Gloucestershire GL5 4EP

www.amberley-books.com

British Library Cataloguing in Publication Data.
A catalogue record for this book is available from the British Library.

ISBN 978 1 3981 0153 1 (print)
ISBN 978 1 3981 0154 8 (ebook)

Typesetting by SJmagic DESIGN SERVICES, India.
Printed in Great Britain.

Contents

Map   4

Key   6

Introduction   7

The 50 Buildings   11

Acknowledgements   96

About the Author   96

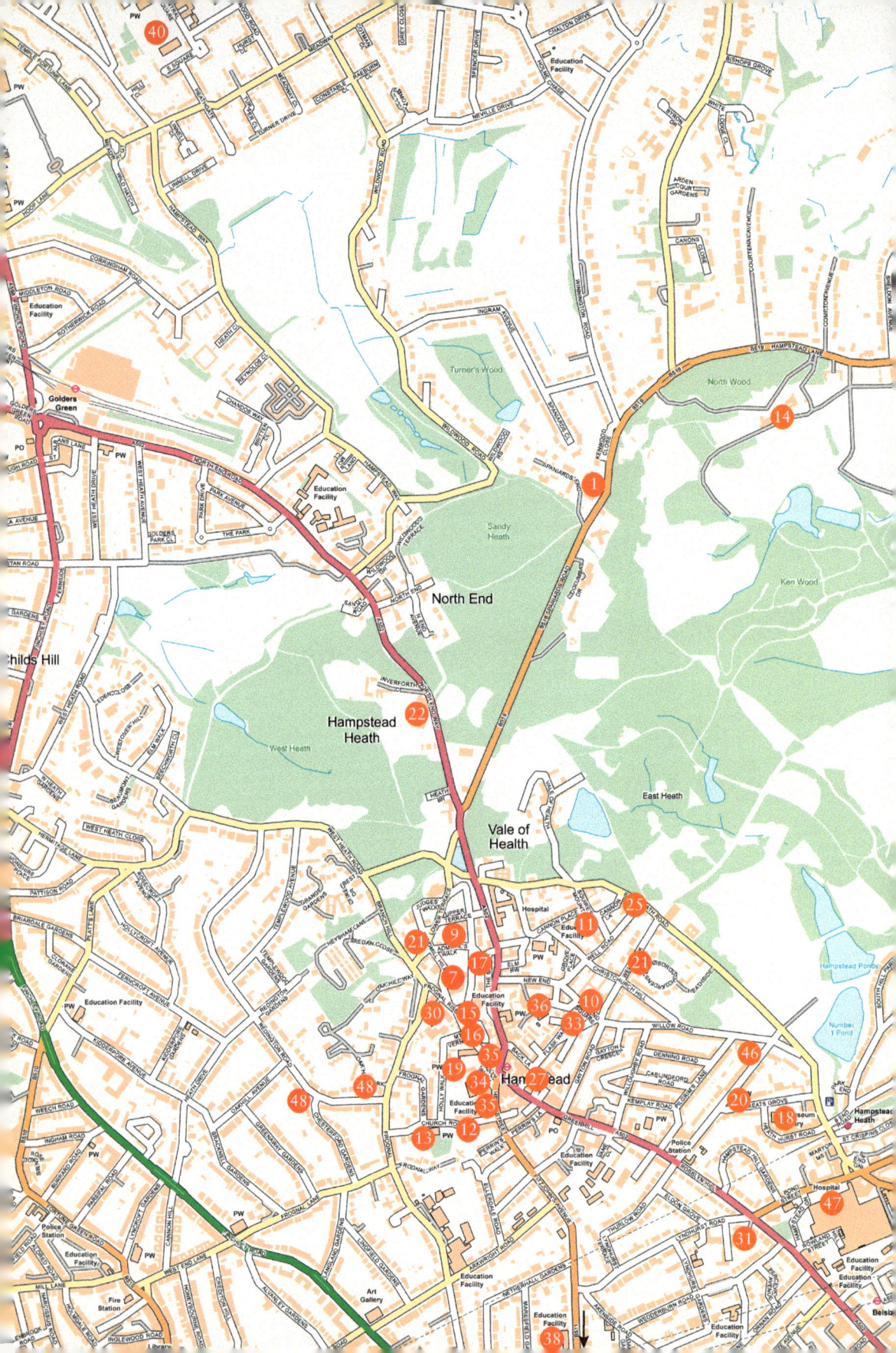

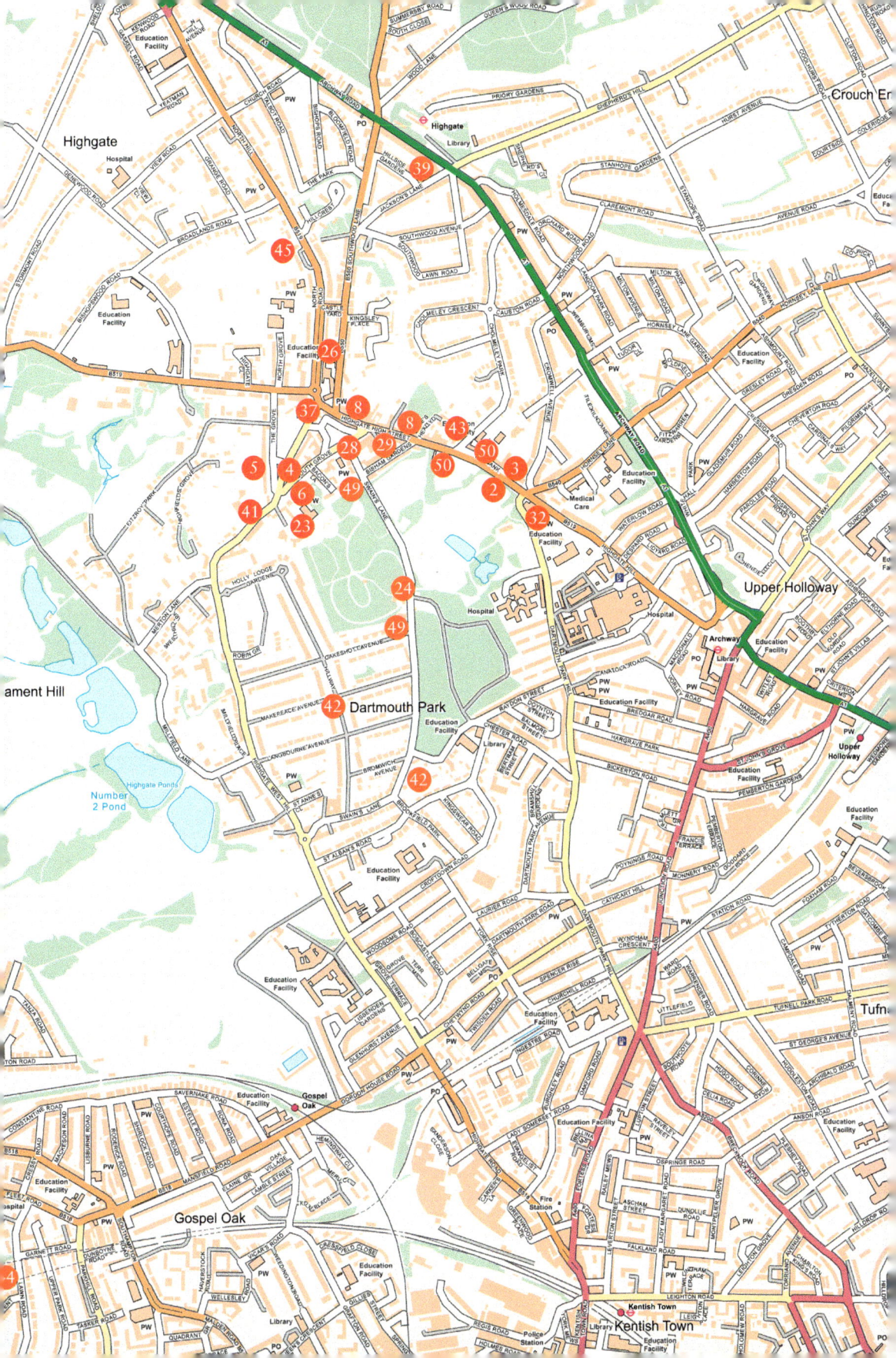

Key

1. The Spaniards Inn, Spaniards Road, Hampstead
2. Lauderdale House, Highgate Hill
3. Cromwell House, No. 104 Highgate Hill
4. The Flask, No. 77 Highgate West Hill
5. Nos 1–6 The Grove, Highgate
6. The Old Hall, South Grove, Highgate
7. Fenton House, Hampstead Grove, Hampstead
8. Highgate High Street and Englefield House
9. Admiral's House and Grove Lodge, Admiral's Walk, Hampstead
10. Burgh House, New End Square, Hampstead
11. Cannon Hall and Parish Lock-up, Nos 14 and 11 Cannon Place, Hampstead
12. Church Row, Hampstead
13. Hampstead Parish Church, Church Row
14. Kenwood House, Hampstead Lane
15. Romney's House, No. 5 Holly Bush Hill, Hampstead
16. Holly Mount and the Holly Bush, Hampstead
17. Old Grove House and New Grove House, Nos 26 and 28 Hampstead Grove, Hampstead
18. Keats House and Keats Grove, Hampstead
19. Holly Walk, Holly Place and St Mary's RC Church, Hampstead
20. Downshire Hill and St John's Church, Hampstead
21. Constable's Houses: No. 2 Lower Terrace and No. 40 Well Walk, Hampstead
22. Inverforth House, North End Way, Hampstead
23. St Michael's Church, South Grove, Highgate
24. Highgate Cemetery, Swain's Lane, Highgate
25. The Logs, Nos 17–20 Well Road, Hampstead
26. Highgate School and Chapel, North Road, Highgate
27. The Flask, No. 14, Flask Walk, Hampstead
28. Pond Square and the Highgate Literary and Scientific Institute
29. Angel Inn, No. 37 Highgate High Street
30. Former Mount Vernon Hospital, Mount Vernon, Hampstead
31. AIR Recording Studios, Lyndhurst Avenue, Hampstead
32. St Joseph's Roman Catholic Church, Highgate Hill
33. Old Bathhouse, No. 36 Flask Walk, Hampstead
34. The Everyman Cinema, No. 5 Holly Bush Vale, Hampstead
35. Heath Street, Hampstead (Fire Station, Hampstead Station and Express Dairy)
36. Former New End Hospital, New End, Hampstead
37. The Gatehouse, Highgate West Hill
38. Freud Museum, No. 20 Maresfield Gardens, Hampstead
39. Jacksons Lane Arts Centre, No. 269a Archway Road, Highgate
40. St Jude's and Free Church, Central Square, Hampstead Garden Suburb
41. Witanhurst, No. 41 Highgate West Hill
42. Holly Village and Holly Lodge Estate, Swain's Lane, Highgate
43. Cholmeley Lodge, Cholmeley Park, Highgate
44. Isokon Flats, Lawn Road, Hampstead
45. Highpoint I and II, North Hill, Highgate
46. No. 2 Willow Road, Hampstead
47. Royal Free Hospital, Pond Street, Hampstead
48. Nos 6, 6.5 and 27a Redington Road, Hampstead
49. Nos 81 and 85 Swain's Lane, Highgate
50. Channing School and the Arundel Centre, The Bank, Highgate

Introduction

Hampstead and Highgate sit on London's Northern Heights, an area of sand and pebble-capped hills and major vantage points from which to view magnificent panoramas of London's skyline. These charming hilltop villages are separated from each other by an enormous green and leafy open space, Hampstead Heath, with Highgate located to the east and Hampstead to the south-west and lie on main routes north from London. For centuries drovers and shepherds herded their sheep and cattle up and down Hampstead and Highgate's steep hills en route to London's Smithfield Market, only interrupting their journey for refreshment or lodging at one of the many inns and taverns on their way. Although many of these have since disappeared, a number still remain along Hampstead and Highgate's main streets. Full of atmosphere, history and fine period features, some – like the Spaniards Inn in Hampstead and The Angel in Highgate – are an excellent reminder of an earlier age with their large yards once used to stable customers' horses.

The two districts have always been renowned for their clean, sweet air – a fact that influenced many of London's citizens, especially the wealthy and powerful, to move to the area away from the capital's dirty and polluted streets. In fact, huge mansions and estates appeared here from as early as the sixteenth and seventeenth centuries, the homes of successful merchants, lawyers, statesmen and aristocrats. While some of these have been demolished and others rebuilt, one or two are still very much part of the fabric of the area, such as Lauderdale House and Kenwood House.

Undoubtedly, Hampstead Heath is a major attraction of the area, with its vast tracts of park and woodland, lakes and abundance of wildlife. Londoners have continuously flocked to the heath to enjoy nature and the countryside, for recreation, and to wonder at the sky and cloud formations. It is no surprise then that so many famous people – writers, poets and artists – have chosen to live here or are associated with Hampstead and Highgate inspired by the beauty of the area and its environment. Evidence of their residency is displayed on very many buildings in the area in the form of English Heritage blue plaques or local heritage plaques.

In the late eighteenth and early nineteenth centuries, artists such as George Romney and John Constable used Hampstead as their base. Romney, nearing the end of his life, only spent three years at his house in Holly Bush Hill while Constable took lodgings here for his family, spending his days sketching, drawing and painting scenes of the heath, the clouds and of the village. In the 1930s Hampstead was a hub for a group of avant-garde artists including Henry Moore, Ben Nicholson, Barbara Hepworth and Piet Mondrian. Many writers and intellectuals have been equally enticed by the delights of the Northern Heights: the Romantic poets John Keats and Samuel Taylor Coleridge lived here in the nineteenth century, and a century later the writers John Galsworthy and J. B. Priestley made it their home. In the 1930s Hampstead and Highgate became a particular magnet for émigrés such as Lubetkin, Breuer, Gropius, Moholy-Nagy and Goldfinger, who fled from Nazi persecution and Eastern Europe, all leading architects of the modern style of architecture so fashionable at the time. Other prestigious Hampstead residents were Dr Sigmund Freud and his daughter Anna who settled in Maresfield Gardens in 1938 and whose house has since opened as the Freud Museum. Unsurprisingly, the area continues to have great appeal: one road in Highgate has consistently been home to famous residents such as the musician Yehudi Menuhin, singers Annie Lennox and George Michael, and the model Kate Moss. In recent times celebrities Jude Law, Liam Gallagher and Jamie Oliver have resided in Highgate while Boy George resides at The Logs, a large Gothic mansion overlooking Hampstead Heath.

Before the early eighteenth century the villages were fairly compact in terms of land and number of residents and, although they grew throughout the 1700s, it was not until a century later that a substantial increase in population occurred. This resulted in a tremendous building boom so that within only a matter of decades Hampstead and Highgate turned into small towns, suburbs of London, with much of their former open spaces and fields covered in elegant Regency and Victorian housing as well as religious and civic buildings. When the railway arrived at Hampstead Heath in 1860 it made a huge contribution to Hampstead's popularity as a day-trip destination, with thousands descending upon the heath, especially on weekends and bank holidays. More access to the main town became available when the Underground opened on Hampstead High Street in 1907. Likewise, the arrival of Highgate's overground railway in 1867 brought great numbers to the area, many of whom came to visit the highly popular Highgate Cemetery on Swain's Lane.

In line with the general expansion from village to London suburb, the nineteenth century was witness to the building of a number of new churches, of entertainment venues, hospitals and schools in every part of Hampstead and Highgate, and many of the buildings are still visible today. During the 1800s St Michael's Parish Church and St Joseph's Roman Catholic Church opened in Highgate while Hampstead's parish church of St John underwent alteration and expansion. Other churches constructed during this time have since become redundant and are now used for different purposes: Waterhouse's magnificent red-brick, Byzantine-style Congregational Church in Hampstead was converted into music recording studios in the 1990s, while Highgate's Jacksons Lane Methodist Church now runs as an arts centre. Likewise, in recent years the former New End and Mount

Vernon hospitals have been transformed into luxury private apartments, New End's former mortuary has become a synagogue and the Express Dairy depot is now a Tesco supermarket.

Both areas today are thriving London suburbs, have high streets that exude an air of luxury and wealth and streets awash with stunning Georgian and Victorian architecture. They are well known for their quaint shops and historic village atmosphere and also for their modernist 1930s housing such as Lubetkin's Highpoint I and II and Wells Coates's Isokon flats.

Highgate has a defined village centre around the original village green, Pond Square, that is characterised by its central space and delightful period houses. It also is home to the Highgate Scientific and Literary Association, the internationally renowned Highgate cemetery (where Karl Marx is buried), and to the Holly Lodge estate, a gated garden suburb. Although Highgate possesses a greater number of older buildings, Hampstead perhaps has the more diverse history as it was once an important eighteenth-century resort known as Wells Spa. A chalybeate spring of natural mineral waters had been discovered here in the late 1690s and was claimed to be the cure for many illnesses and conditions. Hundreds arrived in Hampstead to sample the benefits of the medicinal waters, which led to the rapid construction of lodgings as well as an impressive Assembly Room and Pump Room. In its heyday Wells Spa was considered on a par with Tunbridge Wells; yet, by the mid-eighteenth century its popularity had waned, and its buildings later completely vanished. The only real trace of its former existence now is an impressive stone fountain in Well Walk that commemorates the location of the original spring. Today it is hard to imagine this era as Hampstead has grown so much in size and extends over a wide area that includes the internationally renowned Hampstead Garden Suburb. Lying to the north of the town, it is a very fine example of architecture of the early twentieth century. Yet, Hampstead's old village centre is still apparent in its many tiny streets, alleyways and squares, especially around Hampstead High Street and Heath Street where you can easily stumble across ancient gas lamps, iron gates and railings that all invoke times gone by.

Despite their great similarities each village has its own very distinct character – which is carefully maintained by the local preservation groups and local authorities. In fact, large swathes of Hampstead and Highgate are designated as Conservation Areas, which gives them protection from unapproved or unsightly development. Many of the buildings appear on English Heritage's Register of Listed Buildings recognising their historic and/or architectural significance. This 'listed status' (Grades I, II* and II) ensures that building work must be authorised in advance and that it conforms to the necessary planning regulations. In such a way essential features are protected from loss or damage and buildings preserved for future generations. Interestingly, more than 90 per cent of the buildings covered within these pages are listed buildings and an amazing 20 per cent carry Grade I status. So, a walk around the Northern Heights is certainly a very special

experience and you, the reader, will undoubtedly appreciate what a difficult task
it is has been to select only fifty buildings for the book. There is such a wealth
of interesting buildings, so many stories to tell and truly stunning architecture
that, although frustrated by being unable to include all the buildings I would have
liked, it has been a joy to wander around the village streets and to see, learn and
understand more about these two wonderful villages.

How to Use This Book

In accordance with the 50 Buildings series, the buildings appear in chronological
order according to the time of their original construction.

Please note that the map identifies each building by a number that corresponds
to the numbers used in the text.

Website information for buildings that are open to the public is provided at the
end of each chapter.

The 50 Buildings

1. The Spaniards Inn, Spaniards Road, Hampstead

The Spaniards Inn, perhaps one of London's most notorious pubs, is steeped in legends both about its name and about Dick Turpin (1705–39), the eighteenth-century highwayman. What is known is that it was constructed beside a toll gate at the entrance to the Bishop of London's estate around 1585. Despite many alterations during its lifetime, the Spaniards' main building still exists, with its weatherboarded façade and timber frame. Its historic interior with atmospheric alcoves and oak wood panelling is a delight to visit. Why it is called The Spaniards is a mystery and many theories exist, but no one really knows.

The Spaniards Inn. (Courtesy of A. McMurdo)

The Spaniards Inn and Toll House. (Courtesy of A. McMurdo)

Dick Turpin is said to have eyed up the coaches at the toll gate, marking out which to rob and, having taken the bounty, would make a rapid escape on his trusted steed Black Bess. Although tolls are no longer collected here traffic is forced to slow right down because of the extreme narrowness of the road between the inn and toll gate.

Undoubtedly, a visit to Hampstead is not complete without a trip to the Spaniards Inn – and you will be following in the footsteps of former customers such as Byron, Keats, Shelley and Reynolds. It is an excellent watering hole and a reminder of times gone by.

www.thespaniardshampstead.co.uk

2. Lauderdale House, Highgate Hill

A rare survivor of the Elizabethan age, Lauderdale House was constructed around 1580 and has a long, fascinating history closely associated with eminent and high-ranking individuals. It is one of the borough's oldest properties and has managed to retain much of its original character despite being subjected to numerous changes throughout its almost 450-year existence. Nowadays the house is a much-loved local community arts and education hub and an events venue where art exhibitions, children's activities, live music and theatrical performances

Above and below: Lauderdale House. (Courtesy of A. McMurdo)

are staged. Its commanding position overlooking the magnificent sweeping lawns and terraces of Waterlow Park provides a stunning setting for many weddings and receptions that take place in the house and its grounds.

Designated a Grade II* listed building, Lauderdale House, despite its neoclassic appearance, is an excellent example of a sixteenth-century manor house built partly in the timber-framed tradition with brick foundations. Lauderdale's elegant veranda is lined with Doric columns, and French windows complement its fairly plain exterior. Surrounded by a beautiful eighteenth-century walled garden, the house, grounds and café have become a central meeting point for local residents and visitors.

Lauderdale House is named after its mid-seventeenth-century owner, John Maitland, 2nd Earl of Lauderdale (1616–82), an advisor to Charles I. As a Royalist during the country's Civil War, Lauderdale was confined to the Tower of London in the 1650s and only returned home following Charles II's restoration in 1660. Other occupants of Lauderdale House have included Lord Mayors of London, prominent Quakers, wealthy London merchants and royalty. In 1611 Arabella Stuart, a possible contender to the throne stayed here (and some time later was committed to the Tower, where she died in 1615). Nell Gwynn, the actor and mistress of Charles II also resided at Lauderdale, and it is thought that the king himself would have stayed here with her.

In the late 1880s the house and its estate were given by the then owner, Sir Sydney Waterlow, to the local community. Having suffered a devastating fire in the 1960s it underwent a major restoration and has been managed by the Friends of Lauderdale House ever since.

www.lauderdalehouse.org.uk

3. Cromwell House, No. 104 Highgate Hill

Directly opposite Lauderdale House on Highgate Hill, Cromwell House is an imposing seventeenth-century building that displays an array of fine architectural features, including a striking Victorian cupola. It is one of few Grade I listed properties in the district and is renowned not only for its stunning brickwork façade but also its interior design. The house was constructed in the 1630s for a wealthy London merchant, Richard Sprignell, at a time when Highgate was becoming fashionable due to its clean air and elevated position overlooking the City of London. Although the house was not the work of a famous contemporary architect, the combination of its external features – its Renaissance brickwork, mansard roof, dormers and carved elaborate window brickwork – all indicate a highly skilled designer. Its interior too is splendid and boasts a wonderful Jacobean staircase lined with statues of soldiers and military arms and drums. The *pièce de résistance* on the first floor is undoubtedly the exquisite plaster ceiling of the main salon, bearing a distinct likeness to that found in the Banqueting House in Whitehall.

Cromwell House. (Courtesy of A. McMurdo)

Certainly, Cromwell House was built to be admired and to reflect the position of its owner. In 1675 it became home to the prosperous Jewish merchant Alvaro da Costa, who became the first known Jew to own a property in the country for almost 400 years (following Edward I's expulsion of the country's Jewish population in 1290) and subsequently the area attracted a small Jewish community who prayed at a synagogue within da Costa's house.

The house was sold by the da Costa family in 1749, changing hands several times before being leased to Great Ormond Street Children's hospital in the 1860s to serve as their convalescent home. Following the home's closure in 1924 the house became increasingly neglected and by the 1980s it was in desperate need of restoration. Plans were put forward to convert Cromwell House into luxury apartments, but fortunately the proposals failed to materialise and instead the house interior was restored and adapted for office use. Sold to the Ghanaian High Commission in 1990, it has served as its Passport and Visa Office ever since.

4. The Flask, No. 77 Highgate West Hill

Although a building existed on this site in 1663, the first record of it as The Flask public house dates to 1720. Like many other buildings of its age the pub has undergone considerable change in its life, reflected in its interior eighteenth-century dog-leg stair, wood-panelled rooms, original shutter window bar, twentieth-century bars and exterior wooden porch. Wandering round the pub is an absolute delight as it is full of hidden alcoves and corners and extends across a range of levels. The Flask has great old-world appeal, and its flagstone floors, open fires and ceiling beams all contribute to its cosy atmosphere and feeling of times gone by.

Today it is a Fuller's pub, offering real cask ales, Continental lagers and a diverse selection of wines and spirits. It has become a popular food venue too on account of the fresh seasonal and interesting dishes prepared in its on-site kitchen.

Much history is associated with the building: from its use in the early 1700s as a court of law to it being the venue for one of the country's very first post-mortems (using a body apparently obtained from the nearby Highgate Cemetery). The Flask was also renowned for its 'Swearing on the Horns Ceremony'. In reality this was nothing short of a confidence trick whereby innocent visitors were encouraged

The Flask, Highgate. (Courtesy of A. McMurdo)

to carry out silly acts such as wearing unusual clothes and kissing a pair of ram's horns. In return for their actions, they were promised insignificant, if not worthless, local privileges as Freemen of Highgate. No doubt the locals enjoyed many a laugh before the tradition finally died out during the nineteenth century.

The Flask has always attracted a celebrity clientele; in recent years local residents Kate Moss, Jude Law and Liam Gallagher have been regular visitors, while during the eighteenth and nineteenth centuries the pub was frequented by many an artist or poet including Hogarth, Coleridge, Byron, Shelley and Keats. The pub is also associated with the infamous highwayman Dick Turpin and purports to have not just one but two resident ghosts that haunt its main bar and cellar areas.

www.theflaskhighgate.com

5. Nos 1–6 The Grove, Highgate

The Grove was built around 1688 on the site of the vast garden of a former grand mansion, Dorchester House, and consists of a row of very pretty houses. Sitting at the junction of South Grove and Highgate West Hill, The Grove is set back from the main road and separated from it by a grassy area, adding to the exclusivity of the terrace. Although the six buildings were first constructed as three pairs of semi-detached houses, many alterations have been affected in the intervening years and today Nos 3 and 4 are detached, while Nos 1 and 2 have been converted into one building. All six are listed buildings (Grade II and II*) and display a myriad of striking architectural features both within the houses themselves and in their exterior spaces. Looking at their frontages one can observe marvellous cast-iron and wrought-iron railings, gateways adorned by exquisite period lanterns, wooden hooded doorcases, panelled doors and patterned overlights. The rear gardens, although out of sight, are also listed, containing original seventeenth-century red-brick walls, terraces, parapets, steps and at No. 6 a brick arbour with curved bastions dating to *c.* 1600. Of the six properties No. 4 has undergone the least transformation and still retains its original interior panelling and staircase.

The position of The Grove, at the top of a hill overlooking Hampstead Heath, is magnificent. It is undoubtedly one of Highgate's most desirable addresses and naturally acts as a magnet for the rich and famous. In the 1930s the actress Gladys Cooper and her husband lived in the combined Nos 1 and 2, and in the 1950s Yehudi Menuhin and family moved in here. The poet Samuel Coleridge lived in the attic of No. 3 in the early nineteenth century, and later in the 1930s the house was occupied by the writer J. B. Priestley. More recently it has been home to the supermodel Kate Moss. Her neighbour at No. 5 was the musician George Michael before his untimely death in 2016, and the singer Annie Lennox lived at No. 6 between 1995 and 2005. In recent years celebrity chef Jamie Oliver and actor Jude Law have lived in properties nearby.

Above: Nos 1 and 2 The Grove. (Courtesy of A. McMurdo)

Below left: Nos 3, 4 and 5 The Grove. (Courtesy of A. McMurdo)

Below right: Gateway to No. 5 The Grove. (Courtesy of A. McMurdo)

6. The Old Hall, South Grove, Highgate

From the late 1500s a number of London's nobles and rich merchants bought up land in and around Highgate where they built themselves grand country houses away from the polluted air of the capital. In time, these houses were either substantially altered or rebuilt, and it was not uncommon for parts of the extensive grounds to be sold off to new landowners. Today's 'Old Hall', dating from the early 1690s, was one such building and is a handsome manor house of the period characterised by its brown and red brickwork, a tall central block, high brick walls, and iron entrance gates.

The original house, built for the Cornwallis family in 1588, was set in enormous grounds and was where Sir William Cornwallis (*c*. 1549–1611) entertained Elizabeth I on a number of occasions. Early the next century the house passed into the hands of Thomas, 2nd Earl of Arundel (1585–1646), and then became known as Arundel House. The earl, a great patron of the arts, was a close friend of Francis Bacon (1561–1626), the philosopher and statesman. Sadly, Bacon caught a chill in nearby Swain's Lane while completing an experiment to preserve meat in snow and died at the house in 1626.

The Old Hall. (Courtesy of A. McMurdo)

7. Fenton House, Hampstead Grove, Hampstead

Fenton House is thought to have been constructed in 1693 (a date that appears on one of its chimneystack bricks) and is the oldest surviving mansion in the village. The building's very fine architectural features have earned it Grade I listed status and led to the architectural historian Nicolas Pevsner describing it as one of Hampstead's 'most attractive houses'. It takes its name from Philip Fenton, a Baltic merchant who bought the house in 1793.

In 1952, on the death of its then owner Lady Binning, the house, its contents and walled gardens were bequeathed to the National Trust. An outstanding collection of decorative and fine art had been accumulated by Lady Binning in her lifetime, ranging from sculptures to paintings, Georgian furniture, porcelain, maps and house furnishings. Many of these objects are on display in Fenton House today along with the Benton Fletcher collection of musical instruments (particularly noted for its 1612 harpsichord, once used by Handel).

Right and opposite: Fenton House. (Courtesy of A. McMurdo)

Outside the beautifully cared for gardens extend over three levels and contain a 300-year-old orchard, a sunken rose garden, a kitchen garden, formal lawns, topiary and exotic plantings. Details about the house and its events programme can be found on their website.

www.nationaltrust.org.uk.

8. Highgate High Street and Englefield House

Even though Highgate High Street is a really busy thoroughfare it somehow manages to retain the feel of a small village main street full of diverse, interesting shops, cafés, pubs and restaurants. Unusually, it sits on the boundary of two London boroughs, Camden and Haringey, which have jurisdiction over the south and north sides of the street respectively. Noted especially for its superb display of period residential and retail premises, Highgate High Street contains buildings largely dating to the eighteenth and nineteenth centuries, as well as a few from the late 1600s. The street contains a mix of properties, ranging from tiny cottages, townhouses, terraced housing to ancient shops (some of which are Grade II listed), which exude an aura of quaintness and charm. Several of the shopfronts boast attractive bow windows, while a couple even have their own external canopies (built to protect their goods from exposure to the sun), indicating their original use as butcher's shops.

For centuries cattle and sheep were herded along the street on their way for sale at Smithfield Market in London. This resulted in a dirty and unpleasant thoroughfare

Above and left: Highgate High Street. (Courtesy of A. McMurdo)

Above left: No. 42 Highgate High Street. (Courtesy of A. McMurdo)

Above right: Englefield House. (Courtesy of A. McMurdo)

and made it difficult for local residents to walk along the street. The solution was to construct a high pavement separating pedestrians from the road, and this high-level walkway remains an engaging feature of Highgate High Street today.

Englefield House at No. 23 is a particularly attractive building in the street. Built in 1710 it is easily recognised for its brown and red brickwork, white cornice and prominent red pedimented door. Across the road No. 42, a much more modest house, displays a coat of arms originally placed on a nearby mansion, Ashurst House, before it was demolished in the 1830s. No. 42's owner, a builder, subsequently transferred it to his house – perhaps to give himself greater importance.

Two other notable buildings exist at Nos 44 and 58. The former, once a chemist shop, was where the poet Coleridge acquired drugs for his addiction, and the latter, with its striking white weatherboarded façade and overhanging hoist, was a corn chandlers' premises in its day.

9. Admiral's House and Grove Lodge, Admiral's Walk, Hampstead

Just a stone's throw away from Fenton House (q.v.) these two houses sit cheek by jowl in what today is known as Admiral's Walk (formerly The Grove). They were erected around the same time in the early 1700s and, although semi-detached, have remained separately owned properties. Both houses are designated Grade II listed buildings despite being subjected to a series of alterations and additions since their construction. Admiral's House, the larger of the two, is recognised both for its historic and architectural merits and also for being part of a group of nearby listed buildings. In fact, the house derives its name not from an admiral but rather from a naval captain, Fountain North, who lived here in the late eighteenth century (1775–1811). It was he who extended the original house by constructing a quarter and lower deck, thus giving it the appearance of a ship. It is from the quarter deck that North is said to have fired cannons in celebration of naval victories and royal occasions.

Grove Lodge is a more conventional building: two storeys high and faced in stucco. A plaque prominently displayed on its façade commemorates John Galsworthy (1867–1933), the playwright and writer, who moved into the house in 1918. He was at the pinnacle of his success while living at Grove Lodge and it was here that he wrote his epic work, 'The Forsyte Saga' and received the Nobel Prize for Literature in 1932.

Similarly, Admiral's House bears a plaque to the celebrated nineteenth-century architect, Sir George Gilbert Scott. He was one of the period's most prolific and successful architects and ran an enormous architectural practice – alleged to be the largest in Europe in 1858. He was largely inspired by Pugin (the designer of the Houses of Parliament) and became a passionate supporter of Gothic architecture. Many churches and cathedrals bear his mark, but he is probably best known for his design of St Pancras station and Midland Grand Hotel, the Albert Memorial, and the Foreign and Commonwealth Office. A painting of the house by Constable entitled *The Grove* is on display in Pimlico at Tate Britain.

Admiral's House and Grove Lodge. (Courtesy of A. McMurdo)

Entrance to Admiral's House.
(Courtesy of A. McMurdo)

1C. Burgh House, New End Square, Hampstead

This very fine Queen Anne house dates to 1703–04 and has a fascinating history. Initially built as a modest dwelling for a Quaker couple, it then became home to Dr William Gibbons, physician to Hampstead Spa. It was he who extended the back of the house, installed a library and art gallery on the ground floor along with a staircase embellished with ornate carved tread ends and barley sugar balusters. He was also responsible for introducing the elegant exterior wrought-iron gates that bear his initials. Between 1822 and 1856 the house became the home of Revd Allatson Burgh, after whom it is named. By all accounts he was generally disliked, though locals respected him for campaigning against the lord of the manor's plans to build on Hampstead Heath. Almost a century later Burgh House underwent further expansion when a music room was added at the front of the house. Today this space is frequently hired out for weddings and private functions and is a venue for musical recitals, plays and lectures.

Due to the quality of its many eighteenth-century features and character, Burgh House is now designated a Grade I listed building. It is three storeys high, built of brown brick with red-brick dressings and has a striking five-window symmetrical façade. The interior of the building is equally impressive, containing original fireplaces, dadoes and mouldings as well as fully panelled rooms. Burgh House was somewhat neglected in the late 1800s when occupied by the Royal East Middlesex Militia, but later residents such as art historian Dr George Williamson

Left: Burgh House Terrace. (Courtesy of A. McMurdo)

Below: Burgh House. (Courtesy of A. McMurdo)

took much greater care of it, as is demonstrated by his appointment in 1908 of Gertrude Jekyll to create a new garden for the house.

The local council took over ownership in 1946 and since the late 1970s Burgh House has been leased to a trust, which runs it as a community and arts centre. It is now home to the Hampstead Museum and Art Gallery where you can learn about Hampstead's rich past and see the work of talented local artists. There is a café too with a super outdoor terrace that is much loved by local residents.

www.burghhouse.museumssites.com

11. Cannon Hall and Parish Lock-up, Nos 14 and 11 Cannon Place, Hampstead

The Grade I listed Cannon Hall is a wonderful mansion designed as an early eighteenth-century country house on the outskirts of London. It was built around 1730, has undergone a series of alterations during its existence and today boasts not only six bedrooms but also has a fabulous indoor swimming pool, billiards rooms, library, study and conservatory. The house is set apart from the street behind a high brick wall and fronted by a large courtyard containing the former coachman's house and a low stable block. These buildings join the main house at right angles and are easily identified by an attractive bell turret and weather boarded clock on top of the roof. Cannon Hall itself is a substantial brown- and red-brick building arranged over three floors, with wing extensions at either end dating to the eighteenth and nineteenth centuries. The house acquired its name in the 1830s when Sir James Cosmo Melville, secretary to the East India Company, lived here and had cannons placed along the street. Initially they were used for tethering horses but later took on a new use as street bollards.

Naturally a house of this type has always had great appeal and was the ideal home for the iconic star and actor-manager Sir Gerald du Maurier, who lived here from 1916 to 1934 with his actor wife Muriel Beaumont and their three daughters, Angela, Daphne and Jeanne. All three girls forged successful careers, although Daphne is perhaps the most well known on account of her adventure novels based in Cornwall (such as *Jamaica Inn*, *Rebecca* and *My Cousin Rachel*), some of which later became major movie box office hits.

Cannon Hall itself has associations with filming, having appeared in the 1965 film *Bunny Lake is Missing*, an episode of the 1970s TV series *The Sweeney* and most recently in *Tenet* (2020) starring Elizabeth Debicki and John David Washington.

When the house was first constructed, a magistrates' court filled part of the stable block and there was a parish lock-up built into the garden wall. The lock-up became defunct in 1829 but is still remembered on a black wall plaque at No. 11 Cannon Lane.

Above and left: Cannon Hall. (Courtesy of A. McMurdo)

Below: Parish Lock-up. (Courtesy of A. McMurdo)

12. Church Row, Hampstead

Church Row is considered to be one of Hampstead's greatest gems and is described as its finest and most handsome street in nearly every book written about the area. The majority of its houses were constructed in the late 1720s and hold Grade II listing. Walking along Church Row one cannot help but notice its rich Georgian character, which has been scarcely altered in 300 years. Both sides of the street are lined with houses and unusually there is a narrow central reservation planted with trees that makes it feel more like a square than a street. The houses range between three and five storeys high, are brick built and bear distinctive features of the period. There is much elegant cast-iron work: lamps and lamp brackets, link extinguishers, gates and railings. Several houses have bracketed hooded doorways, canopies and patterned fanlights and others have panelled doors or keystones. What perhaps makes the street all the more attractive is the fact that it lacks uniformity, the houses being of different designs and size, with those on the south side larger than the houses opposite. No. 5 in particular stands out for its weatherboarded frontage and projecting first floor and is a significant contrast to its neighbouring brick terrace.

Church Row. (Courtesy of A. McMurdo)

Above left: No. 5 Church Row. (Courtesy of A. McMurdo)

Above right: Street light in Church Row. (Courtesy of A. McMurdo)

13. Hampstead Parish Church, Church Row

St John-at-Hampstead marks the western end of Church Row (q.v.) adding to its picturesque quality. The present church dates to the 1740s, although there has been a church on this site for around a thousand years. Notable architects were responsible for major extensions and alterations to the parish church in the 1780s and 1840s and in 1878 FP Cockerell (1833–78) reorientated the entire church. This resulted in the altar and chancel being placed at the west end with the main entrance at the east – a highly uncommon layout in England but one that exists elsewhere, as at St Peter's in Rome.

The church itself is classical in design and has a plain brick-built exterior embellished by a square tower and narrow copper spire. The interior bears a distinct resemblance to St Martin's-in-the-Fields in Trafalgar Square with its galleries, loftiness and majestic unfluted Ionic columns. Much of the stained glass was designed by the prestigious glass company Clayton & Bell and there are monuments on the church walls to the poet John Keats and to the dramatist

Right and below: Hampstead Parish Church interior. (Courtesy of Margaret Willmer)

John Harrison's tomb. (Courtesy of A. McMurdo)

Left: John Constable's tomb. (Courtesy of A. McMurdo)

Below: The grave of George Busson du Maurier. (Courtesy of A. McMurdo)

Joanna Baillie. Perhaps St John-at-Hampstead's showpiece is the Henry Willis organ, restored and rebuilt in the 1990s and now returned close to its original 1888 specification.

The church has two graveyards. The older one surrounds St John-at-Hampstead on its western side while the 1812 extension stands separately across Church Row and runs beside Holly Walk. Both contain the graves of many famous people but the best known is probably that of the artist John Constable in a chest tomb with his wife and family, found in the south-east corner of the church graveyard. Nearby is another chest tomb for the clockmaker John Harrison, whose clock solved the problem of 'longitude' measurement in the mid-1700s. In the extension one can visit the graves of George du Maurier, his son Gerald and daughter Sylvia Llewelyn Davies (mother to the five boys that inspired J. M. Barrie's *Peter Pan*). Other notable graves include former Labour prime minister Hugh Gaitskell, actor-manager Sir Herbert Beerbohm Tree, and the architect George Gilbert Scott Jr. Today, these graveyards with their mature landscape are designated as Sites of Importance for Nature Conservation.

www.hampsteadparishchurch.org.uk

14. Kenwood House, Hampstead Lane

It is no wonder that Kenwood House and its grounds are loved and appreciated by so many. Perched up high the house overlooks a landscape of incredible splendour, with sloping lawns, ornamental lake, mature trees and gardens. It has been open to the public since the late 1920s when the house and its art collection were bequeathed to the nation on the death of its owner, Edward Guinness, the 1st Earl of Iveagh.

The first house on the site was built in or around 1616 and still provides the heart of today's far more substantial building. In 1749 an orangery was constructed, and a major renovation of the house was carried out during the 3rd Earl of Bute's proprietorship. Some fifteen years later its new owner, William Murray, Lord Chief Justice (later to become the 1st Earl of Mansfield), commissioned the Adam brothers, Robert and James, to enlarge and redecorate the house for use as his country villa. It was they who built the imposing north entrance portico and remodelled the south front (facing onto the park), adding the low-slung library to the east to balance the orangery to the west. They made massive changes within the house too, transforming it into a stately neoclassic villa. Robert's design for the library was instantly admired for its barrel-vaulted ceiling, Corinthian columns, apses and light décor of pale pastel colours. Although the room is attributed to him, the intricate plasterwork on the ceiling with its series of motifs was the work of Joseph Rose, while the ceiling panels were painted by the Italian artist Antonio Zucchi (also responsible, with Angelica Kauffman, for ceilings and murals within the house).

Above and below: Kenwood House. (Courtesy of A. McMurdo)

Kenwood House service wing. (Courtesy of A. McMurdo)

Kenwood House was extended again in the late 1790s when further wings, a pretty veranda and a new building on the east of the house was constructed housing kitchens and a service wing.

Today, Kenwood House and its grounds open daily, and admission is free. A superb art collection is on display including works by Gainsborough, Vermeer, Romney, Rembrandt and Reynolds and also items of sculpture, furniture and jewellery. There is a shop and an excellent café in the old kitchen block.

www.english-heritage.org.uk

15. Romney's House, No. 5 Holly Bush Hill, Hampstead

George Romney was born in the north of England in 1734 and was apprenticed to a portrait painter as a young man. He later set up a studio in Kendal and built his career by specialising in portraits of the local elite. Before he had even turned thirty, his reputation as a portrait painter was well established and he made the decision to move to London, leaving his wife and family behind. His career continued on its upward curve as he spent many hours painting London's high society – particularly its women. He became one of the country's most highly successful portraitists, considered by many to be among the most celebrated artists of the day. In the early

Above and left: Romney's House. (Courtesy of A. McMurdo)

1780s Romney was introduced to the beautiful Emma Hart (who subsequently became Lady Hamilton and then mistress to Admiral Horatio Nelson), who sat for him regularly and became his muse. Today, the paintings *Emma Hart at Prayer* and *The Spinstress* are on view at nearby Kenwood House (q.v.).

Romney moved into No. 5 Holly Bush Hill in 1797 when he was in his declining years and set about converting it into a home as well as a studio, picture and statue gallery. Sadly, after only three years, ill health compelled him to return to Cumbria back to the wife he'd abandoned many years earlier.

In the early nineteenth century the house was extended by the addition of an assembly room and became popular for its cultural and educational events. It was then converted back to a residence by the architect Clough Williams-Ellis, who lived here between 1929 and 1939. Among other claims to fame, Williams-Ellis is renowned for his design of Portmeirion, the Italianate village in North Wales, made famous by the 1967–68 cult television series *The Prisoner*.

Despite the extensions and changes that have taken place at the property since it was built in 1797 it remains a remarkable example of a house of the period and still retains its pilastered assembly room and geometrical staircase. Nowadays it has Grade I listed building status and is easily identified from the street by its white weatherboarded façade and projecting first-floor bay.

16. Holly Mount and the Holly Bush, Hampstead

Holly Mount is a totally unexpected enclave adjacent to Romney's House (q.v.) that sits high on a hill overlooking London. It is a wonderful tiny hidden street that seems to transport one back to another age. Made up almost entirely of eighteenth- and nineteenth-century Grade II listed buildings it really has the feel of an ancient village lane and has retained much of the original street furniture – cast-iron boot scraper, bollards, railings, chains and lamp posts, most of which

Holy Mount. (Courtesy of A. McMurdo)

The Holly Bush.
(Courtesy of
A. McMurdo)

are also listed. It is undoubtedly one of Hampstead's most picturesque streets and connects to Heath Street and Hampstead village below via long flights of stairs.

Holly Mount is dominated at its entrance by the Holly Bush pub, originally built as the stables for Romney's House and later functioning as a catering wing for the Assembly Rooms. It was converted into a public house in 1928 and is still the most attractive of buildings, with a stuccoed exterior and wooden canopy hood over the main entrance. Visitors love its historic atmosphere, the multitude of rooms and hidden nooks and crannies, hearths, warm wood-panelling and etched glass. Today it is a traditional Fuller's pub, offering customers a warm welcome and excellent food and drink.

www.hollybushhampstead.co.uk

17. Old Grove House and New Grove House, Nos 26 and 28 Hampstead Grove, Hampstead

A brown plaque on the wall of No. 28 Hampstead Grove (New Grove House) reveals that from 1874 to 1895 this was the home of the French-born illustrator and writer George Louis Palmella Busson du Maurier (1834–96). One of the most famous cartoonists of his day, du Maurier worked for the satirical *Punch* magazine for thirty years, coining expressions such as 'bedside manner', 'the curate's egg' and 'good in parts'. In his best-selling book *Trilby* (1894) his heroine wore a distinctive hat, narrow-brimmed, angled at the front and with a slight turn up at the back, which not only became the most coveted fashionable accessory of the time but also introduced the name 'trilby' into the English language. The book was also responsible for another new word: Svengali, the sinister manipulator who had such a hold over the heroine.

Above: New Grove House.
(Courtesy of A. McMurdo)

Right: Old Grove House.
(Courtesy of A. McMurdo)

George du Maurier was Gerald du Maurier's father and grandfather to Gerald's three daughters, Daphne, Angela and Jeanne (q.v. Cannon Hall). When George died in 1896, he was buried in the extension churchyard at the parish church (q.v.) where he was later joined by his daughter Sylvia Llewellyn Davies and her family, his wife Emma and son Gerald.

Although it may look older, New Grove House dates to the eighteenth century. Its 'Tudorisation' took place around 1840 and a series of alterations over the years contributes to its somewhat irregular appearance today. It is a sprawling building, mainly three storeys high and has a square-headed stuccoed entrance that opens directly on to Hampstead Grove. It sits alongside No. 26, Old Grove House, also from the same period and both properties back onto The Mount Square, one of Hampstead's most charming quarters stretching between Heath Street and Hampstead Grove. Old Grove House, like its neighbour, has undergone many changes over the years including several renovations during the twentieth century. At first glance it appears to have more symmetry than New Grove House, but hidden behind its main façade it has a further wing and outbuildings and in earlier times even stables and a laundry (the latter now converted into houses in The Mount Square).

18. Keats House and Keats Grove, Hampstead

Keats Grove is a highly popular locale not only for its association with John Keats (1795–1821) but also for its delightful rural setting so close to Hampstead Heath. Originally called Wentworth Place, its name later changed to Keats Grove in commemoration of the famous poet, although his stay here lasted only two years from 1818 to 1820. Keats had been living close by in Hampstead with his younger brother Tom, but when Tom died of tuberculosis in 1818 Keats moved to Wentworth Place (now No. 10 Keats Grove) into the house of his friend, the writer Charles Armitage Brown. The house, deceptive in appearance, was initially divided into two properties, the other half resided in by the writer and critic Charles Wentworth Dilke. Soon after Keats' arrival Dilke rented out his side to the Brawne family and within a very short space of time the poet had fallen in love with the daughter, Fanny, and they became engaged. Despite her family's objections to the marriage – she was too young and Keats as a poet was not a

Keats House and Library. (Courtesy of A. McMurdo)

Library. (Courtesy of A. McMurdo)

suitable match – plus his own worsening illness (like Tom he was suffering with tuberculosis), Keats managed to produce some of his best poetry at this time, including 'Ode on a Grecian Urn', 'Ode to a Nightingale' and 'La Belle Dame Sans Merci'. In the hope of finding a cure for his health he left Hampstead and travelled to Italy in September 1820, but sadly passed away in Rome the following spring.

In the late 1830s, No. 10 Keats Grove passed to a new owner who converted it into one residence and added a further wing, but took care not to alter the style of the original 1816 house. Now open as the Keats Museum it remains an excellent example of Regency architecture with its white stucco exterior, cast ironwork, slate hipped roof and round-arched window recesses. Perhaps Keats' sojourn in Keats Grove inspired other luminaries to settle here, for No. 20 was once home to the poet and critic Edith Sitwell (1887–1964), No. 11a to the playwright and director Alan Ayckbourn (b. 1939) and No. 12 to former Prime Minister Herbert Asquith (1852–1931).

www.cityoflondon.gov.uk

19. Holly Walk, Holly Place and St Mary's RC Church, Hampstead

Looking down the steep slope of Holly Walk from Mount Vernon one is treated to the most striking view of Hampstead's parish church and London beyond. A particularly narrow street, Holly Walk is lined with pretty houses and leads down to the extension churchyard of St John's Church. There are several small alleys off to the left – Hollyberry Lane, Prospect Place and Benham's Place – that

Above left: Holly Walk and Hampstead Parish Church. (Courtesy of A. McMurdo)

Above right: St Mary's RC Church. (Courtesy of A. McMurdo)

Left: The Watch House. (Courtesy of A. McMurdo)

contain delightful cottages, some dating to the 1790s. A short way down the hill Holly Walk turns into Holly Place where at No. 9 one finds Hampstead's former Watch House. Used by the newly established police force in the early 1830s as its headquarters it is a three-storey building with a semi-basement (probably used as cells) sited at the end of a terrace. The house is easy to spot due to the black wall plaque on its façade that proudly records its former role.

Continuing down the hill one comes across the tiny St Mary's Catholic Church wedged in-between some handsome Georgian houses. The church is, however, a little like Dr Who's TARDIS – much larger within than it appears outside. It was constructed in 1816, before the passing of the Catholic Emancipation Act (1829) that recognised Catholic places of worship, and initially had a rather plain exterior so as not to bring attention to the building. Following the Act, it was re-fronted, and the imposing belfry and sculpture of Virgin and Child were added. A refugee of the French Revolution, Abbe Morel established St Mary's Catholic Church and its early congregation consisted mainly of French refugees.

Step inside the church and you are sure to be surprised: not only is the interior much broader than one expects but there is a long vaulted bright nave that ends at the sanctuary with an outstanding marble baldacchino and tile mosaics. Many residents of Hampstead have taken their wedding vows here, including the author Graham Greene and writer Vivien Dayrell-Browning in 1927 and actors (Dame) Judi Dench and Michael Williams in 1971. During the Second World War General de Gaulle attended Mass here when he was living in nearby Frognal.

www.parish.rcdow.org.uk

20. Downshire Hill and St John's Church, Hampstead

Downshire Hill, as its name suggests, is built on one of Hampstead's many hills and has a superb view of Hampstead Heath along its length. The road is extremely picturesque with many stuccoed villas, enhanced by attractive cast-iron balconies and railings, canopies and bay windows. Most of the buildings date to around 1820 and although many are built in the Regency style (including some Gothic architecture) there is a distinct lack of uniformity. However, this appears not to detract from the overall vista but actually adds to the charm of the road.

St John's Church, Grade I listed, is undoubtedly Downshire Hill's most iconic building, sitting at the junction with Keats Grove. Its marvellously symmetrical west front reminds one of churches on America's eastern seaboard, and stands out on account of its stuccoed exterior, Doric porch, clock and bell cupola. The interior too is most impressive, full of interesting features such as the original wooden pews, a double-staircased vestibule and the Bevington & Sons organ. St John's Church was built between 1818 and 1823 and was from the start a proprietary chapel – maintained by private individuals, financially independent with all costs borne by the congregation. It is one of few such chapels that exist in England today and still receives no funding from the Diocese of London.

Devonshire Hill has always acted as a magnet to those involved in the creative industries and during the early part of the twentieth century it became home to

Above: St John's Downshire Hill. (Courtesy of A. McMurdo)

Left: No. 49a Downshire Hill. (Courtesy of A. McMurdo)

the Hampstead Set of artists including the Carlines, Stanley Spencer and Henry Lamb. Other famous residents include scientist Sir Peter Medawar, actor Dame Flora Robson, and architect Sir Frederick Gibberd. In the mid-1970s a minimalist glasshouse was built at No. 49a by the architects Michael and Patti Hopkins. Although highly controversial at the time, it has since achieved Grade II* listing as one of the earliest examples of high-tech architecture.

No. 13a Downshire Hill. (Courtesy of A. McMurdo)

Downshire Hill also boasts its own pub: the Freemasons Arms. Over 200 years old, it remains a most popular venue offering excellent food, drink and ambiance. Be sure to visit its unusual basement skittle alley – supposedly the last of its type in London today.

www.sjdh.org

21. Constable's Houses: No. 2 Lower Terrace and No. 40 Well Walk, Hampstead

Every summer from the early 1820s John Constable moved his wife and family from their London home to Hampstead so that they could benefit from the good clean country air as well as enjoy the scenery of the wild heathland. He was one of a cohort of artists, such as Hogarth, Romney and Gainsborough, who chose to settle in the northern heights, but unlike the other artists he spent considerable time in Hampstead. It was during the period 1821–37 that he sketched and painted numerous scenes of the heath, the area's trees and flora, the sky and cloud formations as well as some of the district's very large and splendid houses. In fact, one of his earliest works, the *Admiral's House* (q.v.) was finished when he was lodging at No. 2 Lower Terrace between 1821 and 1822, and this painting can still be viewed at Tate Britain in Pimlico.

In 1827 Constable moved into fashionable Well Walk. This was where a century earlier in its heyday as the spa resort Hampstead Wells, ladies and gentlemen took the 'waters', attended the Pump and Assembly Rooms, and promenaded in their finery up and down the narrow streets. Constable's house at No. 40 was fairly modest for the time, but it suited him well and was just a short walk to the heath. Very sadly his wife Maria, consumed with tuberculosis, died within a year of their move and Constable was left to fend alone for their seven children. Despite losing his great love Constable took solace in his art, continuing to draw and paint and produced some of his greatest landscapes of Hampstead before his own death in 1837. He was buried alongside his wife in the churchyard at St John-at-Hampstead (q.v.).

Today a commemorative fountain stands immediately opposite No. 40 Well Walk as a reminder of Hampstead Wells, but the entertainment rooms have long since disappeared. Well Walk itself has remained a highly popular enclave and has attracted many famous figures to live here and in nearby streets including the Poet Laureate, John Masefield, author J. B. Priestley, birth control pioneer Marie Stopes and actors Jeremy Irons and Sinead Cusack.

Below left: No. 2 Lower Terrace. (Courtesy of A. McMurdo)

Below right: No. 40 Well Walk. (Courtesy of A. McMurdo)

22. Inverforth House, North End Way, Hampstead

Perched up high overlooking Hampstead Heath and set in its own extensive grounds, Inverforth House is one of Hampstead's most impressive country houses. First built as Hill House in 1807, it was completely altered in the 1890s and underwent further major modifications when in 1904 it became the property of William Hesketh Lever, proprietor of the soap manufacturing company Lever Brothers. On Lever's death the house was bought by the shipping magnate Lord Inverforth, who bequeathed it to Manor House Hospital in 1956. From this time on it was known as Inverforth House. The estate itself was divided up a few years later when the City of London Corporation took control over a part of the grounds comprising the Hill Garden and pergola. In the late 1990s, Inverforth House, with Grade II listed building status, was redeveloped and today is subdivided into a number of luxury apartments.

During William Lever's tenure many changes were made to the house and its estate; this included the addition of two new wings (one to accommodate his prized art collection), an Ionic veranda, terrace, ballroom and library wing. To enlarge the grounds, he acquired two neighbouring houses and then installed a stunning colonnaded pergola walk leading to his gardens between the house and the heath. This wonderful walkway, full of climbing plants and exotic flowers is today undoubtedly the best place from which to view and appreciate Inverforth House's fabulous garden front and its mainly neo-Georgian architecture.

Inverforth House. (Courtesy of A. McMurdo)

The Pergola. (Courtesy of A. McMurdo)

The Pergola and Belvedere. (Courtesy of A. McMurdo)

In 1922, in recognition of a lifetime of philanthropic works, Lever was elevated to the peerage and became the 1st Viscount Leverhulme. As an employer who believed that happy and healthy workers were the key to a successful business, he had the village of Port Sunlight built on the Wirral Peninsula in the 1880s to provide the workforce with comfortable homes, many of which displayed architectural features associated with William Morris and the Arts and Crafts movement. In addition to their accommodation the residents benefited from well-landscaped open spaces, communal facilities and an art gallery displaying artworks from Lord Leverhulme's own collection of fine and decorative art.

23. St Michael's Church, South Grove, Highgate

The elegant octagonal spire of St Michael's, Highgate, is not only a local landmark, but stands immediately above the western section of Highgate Cemetery (q.v.) dominating the skyline. Built on high ground, the church opened in 1832 and received immediate praise for its neo-Gothic architectural style. Designed by one

St Michael's Church. (Courtesy of A. McMurdo)

of the nineteenth century's most talented architects, Lewis Vulliamy (1791–1871), it can be seen from miles around and is said to be the highest standing church in London – its main entrance is level with St Paul's Cathedral dome's cross.

St Michael's occupies the site of what had once been a great house, built in 1694 for Sir William Ashurst, former Lord Mayor of London. Before the church opened here the villagers and pupils from Highgate School (q.v.) attended services in Highgate Chapel beside the school. However, with a burgeoning population it became increasingly obvious the chapel was too small and, following a lengthy dispute between the school and church in the early 1800s, permission was granted to erect a new parish church elsewhere in Highgate.

Vulliamy's church was designed to seat 1,500 with a small sanctuary, galleries and box pews that extended through the nave and aisles. Within fifty years the box pews and aisles were replaced by open benches, the sanctuary was enlarged, and a central aisle installed. This was the work of another great Victorian architect, G. E. Street (1821–81), the man renowned for his design of the Royal Courts of Justice on the Strand. The third major contributor to the church was the Gothic Revivalist architect Temple Moore (1854–1920), who in the early 1900s was responsible for introducing the statuary and colourful stencilled decoration in the sanctuary.

The interior of St Michael's is remarkably bright and the building is endowed with a very beautiful reredos, tall arcades and mosaic tiled floor. The church's magnificent east window depicts the Last Supper and is a real tribute to the genius and skill of its creator the Irish stained-glass artist Evie Hone (1894–1927). A commemorative slate slab to the much-admired poet and local parishioner Samuel Taylor Coleridge lies on St Michael's central aisle.

www.stmichaelshighgate.org

24. Highgate Cemetery, Swain's Lane, Highgate

The Cemetery of St James at Highgate (known as Highgate Cemetery) opened in the late 1830s and was one of seven 'great' private cemeteries to be established in a ring around London. The cemetery's location, formerly part of the grounds and orchards of Ashurst House, was particularly challenging due to the gradient of its sloping site. However, careful design by its architects, Stephen Geary and, following his death, J. B. Bunning, not only made best use of the land but also resulted in the retention of some of the former estate's attractive ornamental trees and shrubs. Geary, recognising the contemporary fascination with Egypt, designed an Egyptian avenue boasting a monumental gateway flanked by two enormous obelisks. Lined with tombs, the 100-foot avenue crept up the hillside to the Circle of Lebanon, a spot dominated by an enormous cedar tree (only recently replaced due to decay), and surrounded by a round Columbarium. Nearby, brick catacombs were erected on what had previously been the garden terrace of Ashurst House, and these are still in situ. By the early 1850s

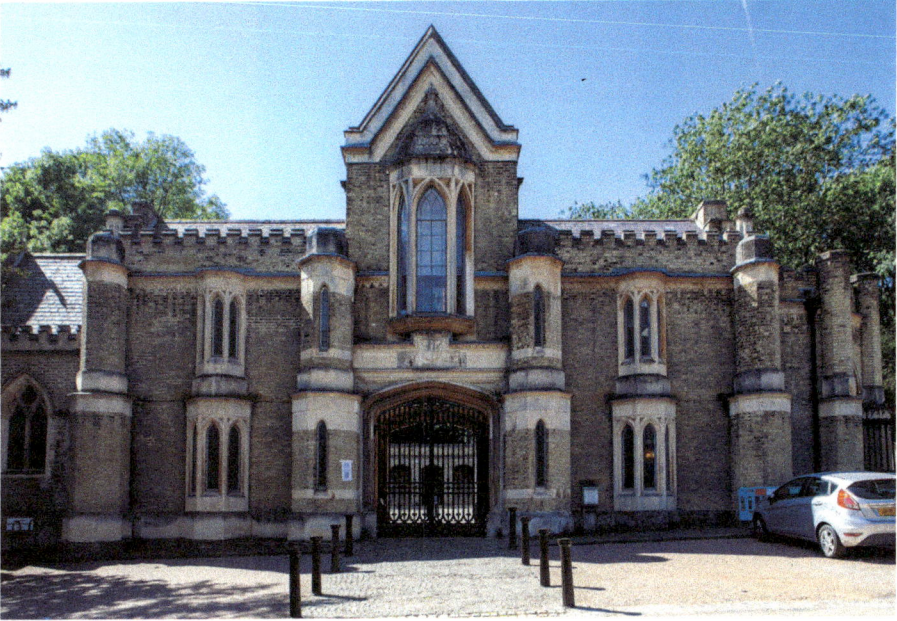

Highgate Cemetery – entrance to the west side. (Courtesy of A. McMurdo)

so many of London's rich and famous sought to be buried here that the cemetery was enlarged by building a cemetery to the east of Swain's Lane.

Today both cemeteries, East and West, are renowned for their range of monuments and tombs, some of which are embellished by animals, sculpture or by architecture. The most elaborate tomb in the West Cemetery, that of the newspaper proprietor Julius Beer (1836–80), sits on top of the hill above the Columbarium

Highgate Cemetery. (Courtesy of A. McMurdo)

and is modelled on the Mausoleum of Halicarnassus, one of the Seven Wonders of the Ancient World. In the East Cemetery the tomb of the political philosopher Karl Marx, easily identified by his large bronze portrait bust, is a site of constant pilgrimage.

Since the 1970s Highgate Cemetery has been managed by the Friends of Highgate Cemetery, who strive to retain its wonderful romantic Gothic atmosphere and

Above left: The Circle of Lebanon. (Courtesy of Friends of Highgate Cemetery Trust)

Above right: The tomb of Karl Marx. (Courtesy of A. McMurdo)

Below left: The grave of Harry Thornton. (Courtesy of A. McMurdo)

Below right: The grave of Patrick Caulfield. (Courtesy of A. McMurdo)

landscape. Within its walls lie the remains of vast numbers of celebrated figures from every walk of life. Artists, media personalities, entrepreneurs, musicians and scientists all rest here, so a stroll around the grounds cannot fail to delight the curious.

www.highgatecemetery.org

25. The Logs, Nos 17–20 Well Road, Hampstead

The Logs must surely be one of Hampstead's most bizarre properties, with its mix of Gothic, Italianate and French chateau features. It is really impossible to ignore as the huge villa sits on a prominent corner at the junction of East Heath Road and Well Road and directly overlooks the heath. Built in yellow and red brick with stone dressings, its façade is full of ornamentation with playful gargoyles, a tower with French-style pyramidal roof and an array of arched and pointed windows. The house was built in the late 1860s for Edward Gotto, a local developer and civil engineer, to what it is said to be largely his own design. Either loathed or loved The Logs has a definite presence, and visitors standing outside the gabled stone gateway in Well Road will marvel at the animals that adorn its archway.

Interestingly, a number of well-known figures have occupied the house during its 150-year existence, including Thomas Crapper, who made his name by inventing the flush toilet. More recently in the 1960s The Logs was home to Marty Feldman, the comedy writer and actor renowned for his bulging eyes, and since the 1980s to the flamboyant singer and songwriter Boy George.

Left and previous page: The Logs.
(Courtesy of A. McMurdo)

26. Highgate School and Chapel, North Road, Highgate

The imposing school buildings and chapel sitting at the northern end of Highgate High Street form an excellent backdrop to Highgate village, bringing much character to the area. Designed in the mid-1860s by the architect Frederick Pepys Cockerell (1833–78), the warm red-brick Gothic buildings are a real focal point at the junction of Hampstead Lane, Highgate High Street and North Road. Set back from the road behind elegant black iron memorial gates the school sits adjacent to the chapel, which is famed for its windows, clock tower and graceful spire.

The original Highgate School was founded in 1565 by Sir Roger Cholmeley (1485–1565), a lawyer who had served as Lord Chief Justice of England under three Tudor monarchs (Henry VIII, Edward VI and Mary I) and was a major local landowner. The school opened in the late 1570s on land that was previously home to a hermitage chapel. It offered free grammar school education to forty local poor boys and consisted of a schoolroom and chapel, the latter to service both the scholars and local residents.

In time, the chapel became too small and following a court judgement in the 1820s it was demolished. A new parish church of St Michael's (q.v.) was erected in South Grove entirely for the use of local residents. It was not until 1867 that a new chapel was built at the school during John Bradley Dyne's tenure as headmaster. Under his direction the school underwent much change and by the

Above: Highgate School. (Courtesy of A. McMurdo)

Left and previous page bottom: Highgate School Chapel. (Courtesy of A. McMurdo)

time he retired in 1874 it had taken on all the characteristics of an English public school preparing pupils for university and professional careers.

For more than 400 years Highgate School operated as a single-sex school, but since 2004 it has opened its doors to both boys and girls. Unsurprisingly, many famous figures have passed through its classrooms. Old Cholmelians (former pupils of Highgate) include the politician Anthony Crosland, historian Martin Gilbert, inventors Sir Clive Sinclair and Revd John Venn, Poet Laureate Sir John Betjeman, architect Sir Reginald Blomfield, fashion designer Hussein Chalayan MBE and composers Sir John Taverner and John Rutter CBE.

27. The Flask, No. 14, Flask Walk, Hampstead

The Flask is one of Hampstead's most popular pubs that attracts a clientele from far and wide. Its current building is late Victorian (1874) and replaced an earlier tavern on the site that was known for a time as the Thatched House because of its roof. Prior to this it was called the Lower Flask to distinguish it from the Upper Flask that sat at the top of Hampstead Hill on East Heath Road. It had acquired the name 'Flask' in the late 1690s when chalybeate mineral waters were discovered at nearby Well Walk and the pub became a kind of bottling plant, where flasks were filled with the medicinal water. The flasks, at a cost of threepence were then sold to wealthy customers in the City of London. They were highly sought after despite the so-called nasty metallic taste of the water and people were lured into believing the marketing hype that drinking the water would cure all manner of ailments especially gout, shingles, bladder and kidney problems. It was a time when spa resorts were particularly fashionable and Hampstead Wells' spring water was deemed to be as beneficial as that of famous Tunbridge Wells. In time however, the attraction of the spring water diminished, and the pub reverted to its original role as a tavern, becoming a major part of village life. During the eighteenth and nineteenth centuries when Flask Walk was a working-class area there were several shops and cottages beside the pub, giving it the appearance of a small high street, and by the late nineteenth century it was home to two bakers, butchers and fishmongers as well as an ice-cream maker, tailor, tobacconist and leather seller.

The pub was completely rebuilt in 1874 and much of its original decoration – the colourful patterned tiles, cast-iron fireplaces, mahogany bar counter and wall panelling, as well as its etched glass partition – can still be seen today. Inside there are three bars and a conservatory extension for dining. The Flask has been owned by Young's Brewery since 1904 and is recognised by CAMRA (Campaign for Real Ale) as a London Historic Pub.

www.theflaskhampstead.co.uk

The Flask, Hampstead. (Courtesy of A. McMurdo)

Flask Walk. (Courtesy of A. McMurdo)

28. Pond Square and the Highgate Literary and Scientific Institute

Pond Square, just a stone's throw away from Highgate High Street, is to all intent and purposes Highgate's village green even though there is scarcely any grass and no water! The ponds here disappeared over 150 years ago, but the square, famed today for its towering plane trees, remains Highgate's central hub and has been an official open space since 1884. It is where the annual summer Highgate Fair takes place, an afternoon full of activity and family entertainment and the spot where locals gather for carol singing in December. The square, although not homogenous is lined with attractive properties, many of which date to the eighteenth century. However, both older and younger houses are interspersed along its sides and this is what gives Pond Square so much character.

Pond Square is in fact triangular in shape, with one side, South Grove, leading into Highgate High Street. Facing the square along South Grove are a group of substantial buildings (Nos 10, 10a and 11), nowadays home to the Highgate Society and the Highgate Literary and Scientific Institute. These are listed buildings that not only display wonderful period features but also possess a great deal of history. No. 10, Church House, set behind iron railings, is a double-fronted red and brown brick detached house built in the early 1700s. A century later the house was used as a private school, but by the 1920s was home to Harry Beck

The Highgate Literary and Scientific Institute. (Courtesy of A. McMurdo)

(1902–74) a draughtsman who designed the London Underground map. An annexe (10a) was added to the building in 1848 and it is here today that the Highgate Society, largely involved with planning issues, is based. It works hard to protect and enhance Highgate's amenities and maintain village attractions.

Immediately next door at No. 11 is the Highgate Literary and Scientific Institute, which opened here in 1839. It is one of few such institutes to have survived into the twenty-first century and remains a remarkable resource for Highgate providing an excellent well-stocked library as well as a programme of lectures, debates, concerts and exhibitions. It is very much at the heart of Highgate's cultural scene.

www.hlsi.net

29. Angel Inn, No. 37 Highgate High Street

As Highgate lies on the key route north from London it comes as no surprise that Highgate High Street has always been full of coaching inns and taverns. For centuries it was a major stopping point for travellers on journeys into and out of London. After many hours spent on the road, Highgate was considered to be the ideal place to rest and freshen up before the final passage into town. From written records Angel Inn is known to have existed since at least 1610, and one can assume that with such an enviable location, beside Pond Square and at the very heart of the village, it received many customers. Travellers' horses were cared for beside the inn in Angel Yard where they would be fed, watered and stabled overnight. The stables have long since gone, although Angel Yard itself remains and is a wonderfully atmospheric setting that is characterised by its original cobbled paving and an old stone block used for mounting a horse. Originally the yard contained a number of buildings (including a coach house and cottages), but by the early 2000s their condition had deteriorated to such an extent that it was decided to restore and convert them into four individual units. Fortunately, this work was carried out most sympathetically, which has ensured the character of Angel Yard allowing visitors to get the feel of Highgate's coaching inn past.

Today's pub dates to 1930 and is neo-Georgian in style. It is a handsome building of red brick, two storeys high with dormers and a central main doorway flanked by three windows on each side. The interior is made up of a single room full of period and contemporary furnishings and has a lovely cosy ambiance (an open fire rages in winter). The Angel serves cask ales and craft beers and offers a wide menu catering to all tastes.

Outside the pub a small plaque remembers Graham Chapman (1941–89) of Monty Python fame who, along with the rest of the gang, was a regular here in the 1970s. It describes him as 'a very naughty boy' who 'drank here often and copiously'.

www.theangelhighgate.co.uk

Angel Inn. (Courtesy of A. McMurdo)

3c. Former Mount Vernon Hospital, Mount Vernon, Hampstead

Mount Vernon Hospital began life as a treatment centre for tuberculosis (TB) and was established as the North London Hospital for Consumption and Diseases of the Chest in 1860. It was originally located in Fitzroy Square in London at a time when TB was a deathly disease and still rampant in society, threatening many Londoners' lives. While the wealthy could travel abroad to find cures at Continental sanitoriums, this was not an option for the majority of the population, so the construction in 1880 of a specialist hospital at Mount Vernon was highly welcomed by the local community.

A donation of £200,000 was provided for its construction by Charles Dunell Rudd (1844–1916), a millionaire and director (along with Cecil Rhodes) of the De Beers Mining company, whose mother and first wife had succumbed to the disease. The huge hospital, which looks much like a French Renaissance chateau, was designed by Thomas Roger Smith, an architect and Professor of Architecture at University College London who favoured European styles of architecture. Built in stages, the hospital, renowned for its new and modern methods of treatment for TB (ensuring patients received plenty of fresh air and exercise), continued to increase in size and ultimately its bed capacity grew from 34 to 140 in just over twenty years. In 1913 before the outbreak of war the governors closed the hospital site, patients were transferred to Mount Vernon Hospital in Northwood and the buildings became home first to the National Institute for Medical Research, and after 1980 to the National Institute for Biological

Former Mount Vernon Hospital. (Courtesy of A. McMurdo)

Standards and Control. In the 1990s the entire complex was redeveloped and converted into high-end apartments and housing selling for several million pounds.

Beside the hospital buildings in Mount Vernon and practically concealed by a boundary wall is the attractive Georgian Grade II listed Mount Vernon House. This was where two directors of the National Institute for Medical Research, Sir Henry Dale (1875–1968) and Sir Peter Medawar (1915–87) lived for some of their tenure. Both men received knighthoods and were awarded the Nobel Prize: Dale, for Medicine in 1936 and Medawar for Physiology in 1960.

31. AIR Recording Studios, Lyndhurst Avenue, Hampstead

Based in what was once a congregational church the recording studios were the creation of Sir George Martin (1926–2016), musician, composer, arranger and most importantly record producer. It was he who discovered and signed up the Beatles to EMI in 1962 and became producer to a list of 1960s and 1970s artists such as Elton John, Cilla Black, Gerry and the Pacemakers and John Williams. Martin established Associated Independent Recordings (AIR) with three other top record producers in 1970. They introduced the concept of freelance record production whereby the cost of new releases would be borne by AIR rather than

Above and opposite: AIR Recording Studios. (Courtesy of A. McMurdo)

the record labels themselves, with AIR receiving royalties on sales made. This was not simply a change to the way the music business operated but one that was hugely successful. AIR grew from strength to strength in the next twenty years, with studios in Oxford Circus and in the Caribbean. Looking for new premises in the early 1990s Sir George came across Lyndhurst Hall in Hampstead and immediately recognised its potential to become AIR's new home. A major transformation of the building then took place and AIR Studios Lyndhurst opened for business in 1992.

Lyndhurst Hall is a magnificent red-brick building standing at the junction of Rosslyn Hill and Lyndhurst Avenue. It was built as a church in 1884 by Alfred Waterhouse, the architect who designed the Natural History Museum in South Kensington. Although there are similarities between the two buildings (both have red brickwork and terracotta dressings) the church was built in the Romanesque style with rounded arches, which is quite unlike the museum's Gothic architecture. The impressive and vast church exterior is laid out in an irregular hexagonal plan characterised by a roof full of tiled gables, a lantern and a round-arched entrance. Its interior, hexagonal in shape, has been divided into a concert hall and recording studios since AIR's occupation of the former church. The building's superb acoustics have led to the recording of numerous Oscar-winning and nominated orchestral works, film and TV scores here including *Atonement*, *The Grand Budapest Hotel*, *Mary Poppins Returns*, *Interstellar* and *Sherlock*.

32. St Joseph's Roman Catholic Church, Highgate Hill

The attractive copper green domes of St Joseph's Church are not only a local landmark but can be seen for miles around. The vast building dates to the late 1880s and occupies a corner plot on Highgate Hill near to Waterlow Park at its junction with Dartmouth Park Hill. Following the country's re-establishment of the Roman Catholic hierarchy in 1850 and a growing Catholic population in the neighbourhood, the Catholic Passionists purchased this piece of land to build their mother house for the Passionists in England. Their first church was very quickly replaced, having outgrown the needs of its increasing congregation (largely local Irish immigrants who worked on railway, canal and building construction), and the present church opened in 1889, designed by Albert Vicars in Romanesque and Byzantine styles.

St Joseph's today is a Grade II* listed building on account of its many outstanding features. The west front is particularly distinctive with its rose window and tympanum full of statues. Inside, the church boasts a striking barrel-vaulted

Italian nave as well as a sanctuary decorated with an exquisite baldacchino, Sicilian marble altar and alabaster reredos – all of which benefit from streams of light filtering down through the lantern above.

www.stjosephshighgate.org.uk

Right, below and opposite: St Joseph's Roman Catholic Church. (Courtesy of A. McMurdo)

33. Old Bathhouse, No. 36 Flask Walk, Hampstead

The Old Bathhouse proudly bearing the inscription 'The Wells and Campden Baths and Wash-houses 1888' lies just behind the small grassy area of Flask Walk Green and always arouses the interest of passers-by. The building seems somewhat incongruous in what is now a wealthy quarter of Hampstead, but during the nineteenth century when the neighbourhood had a large working-class population many had no access to a bath or running water at home and there was a pressing need for such an amenity. Hampstead's baths, built by a local landowner, The Wells and Campden Charity, contained nine baths, a laundry and drying room. The baths and wash houses remained in use for almost ninety years until the building was sensitively converted into two residential properties in the 1980s. At the time of writing, one of the two houses is on the market for £2.6 million, a price that demonstrates how much the demographics of the area have changed in just over a century.

It is certainly interesting to see how many historic buildings across the country are being repurposed rather than demolished. The bathhouse's redevelopment is especially heartening when one considers that nothing stands today of the spa buildings of nearby Hampstead Wells visited by so many in the 1700s.

Old Bathhouse. (Courtesy of A. McMurdo)

34. The Everyman Cinema, No. 5 Holly Bush Vale, Hampstead

The Everyman Cinema has had its share of ups and downs in its almost ninety-year history, but it is still one of Hampstead's best-loved venues and retains a most loyal clientele. The building erected in honour of Queen Victoria's Golden Jubilee was opened in the late 1880s as a community centre and Assembly Rooms but later acquired the name 'Hampstead Drill Hall' as Hampstead's volunteer regiment was based here. However, by 1920 its role had changed, and the Everyman Theatre was born, renowned not only for launching new plays and playwrights but also for producing works of George Bernard Shaw and Noel Coward. Its initial success faded and by the early 1930s it was facing financial ruin, which led to the theatre's closure in late 1933. Fortunately, local solicitor and film aficionado James Fairfax-Jones took over the building and converted the Everyman into a 245-seat cinema. From the start Fairfax-Jones was a hands-on proprietor who quickly recognised the popularity with his audience of foreign films. He thus made it his policy to regularly screen such movies and his strategy proved so successful that it marked out the cinema from its competitors and enhanced the Everyman's reputation. With its bold repertoire, low-cost seats and offer of art house programmes, queues stretched outside the cinema attracting filmgoers from every part of London.

During the 1950s the cinema underwent refurbishment when a Cinemascope screen and a small art gallery in the foyer were introduced. However, as the

The Everyman Cinema. (Courtesy of A. McMurdo)

years passed by, the steady decline in audience numbers resulted in the cinema eventually closing its doors. It was then taken over by the entrepreneur Daniel Broch who reopened the cinema as the 'Everyman Hampstead' in 2000, having converted the former bohemian art house from one screen into two. He installed cosy armchairs and sofas in each auditorium and totally redecorated the cinema interior, transforming it into a plush, luxurious venue. Today, a visit to the Everyman Hampstead is no longer cheap but it is certainly a classy experience where blockbuster movies are seen in deluxe surroundings – a world away from the Everyman's earlier indie flea-pit days.

www.everymancinema.com

35. Heath Street, Hampstead (Fire Station, Hampstead Station and Express Dairy)

Heath Street is one of two major arteries running through Hampstead's town centre and is loved for its eclectic collection of shops, cafés, pubs and restaurants. At its northernmost point is Whitestone Pond beside Hampstead Heath from where it descends steeply to its junction with Hampstead High Street before levelling off and meeting Fitzjohn's Avenue. The upper section of Heath Street is narrow and windy and perhaps gives one a taste of times gone by when horses would have plodded up and down the lane through the village and on into London. Although no longer functioning as a pub the imposing, listed four-storey Horse and Groom remains a major landmark here and is a reminder of Hampstead's once thriving tavern trade.

At the foot of the hill is another iconic building: Hampstead's former fire station, which opened in 1874 and was designed by the architect and civil engineer George Vulliamy (1817–1886). Constructed in red brick, it is an eye-catching Gothic building with its own tall clock tower. The tower, originally built to store water, was used as an observation post during the First World War because of its position and height. After the war, however, the fire station closed and was then converted into office space.

Immediately opposite is the entrance to Hampstead station, which, at 58.5 metres, is the deepest Tube station in London's Underground network and considered to be a marvel of engineering when it was constructed in 1907. The Underground Electric Railway Ltd's (UERL) architect Leslie Green (1875–1908) was responsible for its design and it is a typical example of the brand he created for the company with its ox-blood tile exterior and art nouveau details within. Unsurprisingly, the station's deep tunnels became a safe haven for many locals sheltering from overhead bombing during the Second World War.

A further building of note at Nos 23–27 Heath Street (now a Tesco) was once home to the Express Dairy Company Limited. It was to these purpose-built

Above and right: The former fire station. (Courtesy of A. McMurdo)

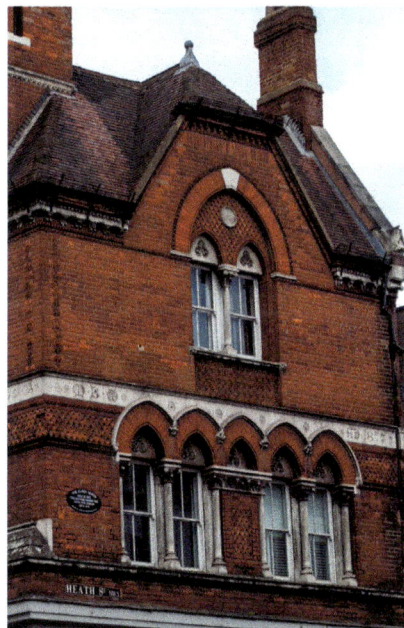

The former Express Dairy. (Courtesy of A. McMurdo)

premises that milk was delivered by train from farms outside the capital and then distributed on milk carts around the local area – far different to a trip to the local supermarket today!

36. Former New End Hospital, New End, Hampstead

New End Hospital began life in 1869 as the infirmary to Hampstead Workhouse, a building that had existed on the site since 1800. The workhouse was rebuilt in the mid-nineteenth century as the original buildings outgrew their use and additional blocks were erected in the 1880s when new wards were added, and a laundry and boiler house built. Today, the decorative, tall red-brick and stone chimney is all that remains of the boiler house, but it is such a rare example of its type that it carries Grade II listed building status. Likewise, the Circular Ward block and water tank tower designed by Charles Bell in 1884 are listed buildings (Grade II*). The ward tower is of particular historic significance; proposed in a paper written in the 1870s by John Marshall, Professor of Surgery at University College Hospital, it was the first detached circular ward tower to be built in the country.

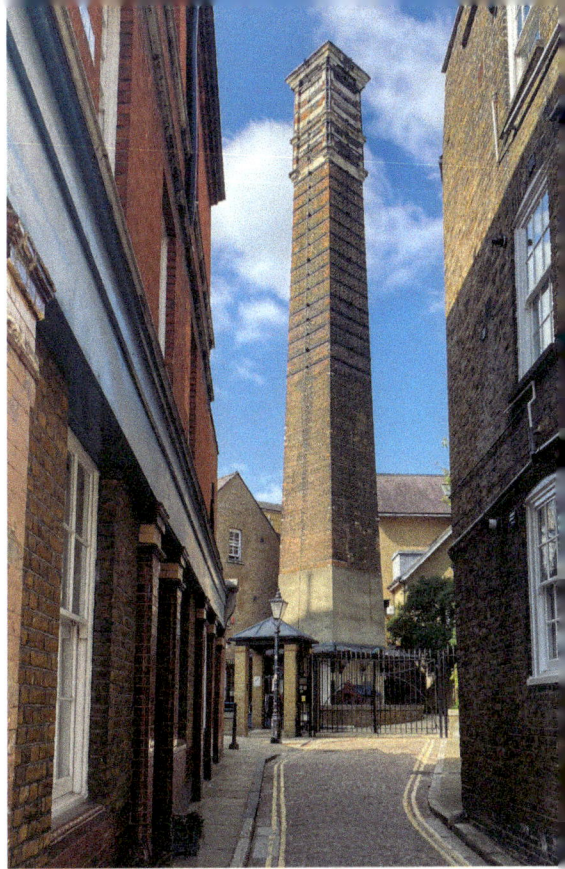

Right: Chimney of New End Hospital. (Courtesy of A. McMurdo)

Below: Former New End Hospital. (Courtesy of A. McMurdo)

Former mortuary of New End Hospital. (Courtesy of A. McMurdo)

Its three floors had twenty-four hospital beds arranged radially around the walls. Tall windows were placed at regular intervals between the beds providing patients with excellent cross-ventilation and a great deal of natural light.

The workhouse and hospital were commandeered for military use during the First World War, but the hospital reverted to its previous role in 1922 and was from then on known as New End Hospital. In 1930 it became a general hospital and established its reputation as a centre for endocrinology. By the late 1960s it was part of the Royal Free Hospital Group and gradually moved its acute services over to the new purpose-built Royal Free Hospital, concentrating on geriatric care. New End Hospital finally closed in 1986 after which planning permission was given to convert its premises into a gated residential housing complex. Although some new buildings were added to the development at that time (such as Young's Court), most of the older hospital wards and ancillary buildings underwent a total transformation and were converted into luxury apartments.

The façade of the original 1849 workhouse still stands on New End and faces the former hospital mortuary, which after its closure became the New End theatre and is now a local synagogue.

37. The Gatehouse, Highgate West Hill

Another of Highgate's landmark buildings, The Gatehouse, has a history going back hundreds of years. Today it is an independently run pub and restaurant that is renowned for its top-class British seasonal cuisine, range of craft beers and international wine list. When the Gatehouse was part of JD Wetherspoon's portfolio (1993–2015) it leased out the first floor of the building to a theatre group named Upstairs at the Gatehouse, which has remained there ever since. The theatre has now become a permanent fixture and is one of London's most loved and popular fringe theatres, staging musicals, drama as well as cabaret to full audiences.

The pub's present building is characterised by its half-timbered mock-Tudor architecture and dates to around 1905. It is one of a series of public houses to have occupied the site but there is nothing written before 1670 that confirms when it first opened here. It is highly probable that the Gatehouse is the oldest of all Highgate's inns due to its position at the entrance to the bishop of London's hunting park and beside the toll gate. From the fourteenth century any traveller wishing to use the road crossing Bishop's Park between Highgate and Finchley had to pay a toll here. The practice was later continued by the lord of the manor until finally all such tolls were abolished and the toll gate itself was demolished in 1892.

The Gatehouse. (Courtesy of A. McMurdo)

Parish boundary marker on the gatehouse wall.
(Courtesy of A. McMurdo)

For much of its life the Gatehouse has been much more than just an inn – a meeting house, courtroom, Victorian Music Hall and even a cinema – and in the early 1900s it attracted customers from all over London for its huge lunches known as 'shilling ordinaries'.

Until fairly recently the borough boundary ran through the pub, which meant that one part came under Hornsey (now Haringey) and the other under St Pancras (now Camden), and one can see parish markers on the Gatehouse's exterior wall with the inscription: 'Hornsey Parish 1859; S.P & P 1791'. Since the boundary moved in 1993 the building falls solely within the London Borough of Camden and is subject to its control.

www.thegatehousen6.com

38. Freud Museum, No. 20 Maresfield Gardens, Hampstead

The founder of psychoanalysis, Sigmund Freud (1856–1939), moved into No. 20 Maresfield Gardens with his family in the summer of 1938, having fled Nazi persecution following the annexation of Austria. When he arrived in Hampstead he was an elderly man and had been suffering from cancer for many years. Despite his poor health Sigmund continued to work in his new home, writing another book, *Moses and Monotheism*, and seeing patients for analysis. He was especially fortunate in being able to bring his collections of art, antiquities, literature and furniture to his new home and thus surrounded himself with familiar objects, which

Freud Museum. (Courtesy of A. McMurdo)

made his life in exile more bearable. Sadly, his illness worsened and despite his daughter Anna's support and nursing he died within the year. Anna (1895–1982), herself a leader of child psychoanalysis, remained in the house until her death in 1982 and it was at her bequest that the house was later turned into a museum.

A visit to the Freud Museum gives a remarkable insight into the lives and work of both Sigmund and Anna Freud. Sigmund's iconic psychoanalytic couch is still very much the centrepiece of his study and visitors delight not only in this but also in his art collections and personal library. Examples of antiquities are found on Sigmund's desk and in cabinets all over the study and the walls are lined with pictures and bookshelves. The house contains many paintings, including portraits of Freud by Salvador Dali and by Ferdinand Schmutzer as well as a couple of paintings by one of Freud's most noted patients, Sergei Pankejeff, known as the *Wolf Man*.

Not only does the museum chart Sigmund Freud's history but there is a room upstairs dedicated to Anna where one can see her analytic couch and discover more about her pioneering work with children. It is a fascinating museum to visit both for its presentation of the lives of father and daughter and for the objects on display. If time allows do explore the garden, which remains much as it was when Sigmund lived here. For details of opening times see their website.

www.freud.org.uk

39. Jacksons Lane Arts Centre, No. 269a Archway Road, Highgate

It seems quite fitting that a centre for the creative and performing arts should have its home in this Gothic-style building, so full of space and character. Designed by local architect W. H. Boney, it opened as a Methodist church in 1905 and immediately became a prominent feature of the area for its pointed arches, steep pitched roof and warm red-brick and stone exterior. When the church closed in the early 1970s a group of local residents began a campaign to transform the building into a community arts hub, a place where people of every age, socio-economic and ethnic background could come and try out their creative skills. In 1975, following the go-ahead from Haringey Council, Jacksons Lane Arts Centre (JLAC) was set up by Nicky Gavron, Melian Mansfield and Paul and Jan Brooker. Funds were then raised so that a theatre and performance spaces could be built for the new venture. From the outset JLAC aimed to support emerging and young artists at the start of their careers, especially working with youngsters in North London's most deprived areas. It offered a range of courses for both adults and children covering the performing arts, comedy and, more unusually, circus.

Today, the centre is the UK's major supporter and producer of contemporary circus, an art form that uses both established and new techniques on the ground and in the air and is sometimes accompanied by music and dance. Thousands of people pass through the JLAC each week to participate in, perform or watch circus acts and the centre commissions artists showcasing their work in the theatre and also on tour around the world. It runs several festivals throughout the year, including the summer Postcards Festival, which offers a programme of

Jacksons Lane Arts Centre. (Courtesy of A. McMurdo)

Jacksons Lane Arts Centre. (Courtesy of A. McMurdo)

circus, cabaret and performance and sponsors the Total Theatre Award for Circus at the Edinburgh Fringe Festival. Many famous names have started their career or performed at JLAC, including David Walliams, Matt Lucas and Eddie Izzard as well as companies such as Complicite, Shared Experience and Out of Joint.

After a period of closure JLAC has recently reopened and now offers even better and more modern rehearsal and studio spaces.

www.jacksonslane.org.uk

4c. St Jude's and Free Church, Central Square, Hampstead Garden Suburb

These two splendid churches dominating Central Square's hilltop are the work of the celebrated English architect Sir Edwin Lutyens (1869–1944), famous for the Cenotaph in Whitehall and his war memorials in northern France. They were constructed between 1908 and 1911 to provide a centrepiece for the newly established Hampstead Garden Suburb and were built facing one another across a large grassy area. The establishment of Hampstead station in the early 1900s led to people moving out of central London into the recently formed suburbs, a fact recognised by the social reformer Henrietta Barnett. She believed that the time was ripe to build a garden suburb where people from all classes could live in an attractive environment and in social harmony and, together with her husband, Canon Samuel Barnett, and a group of other like-minded people set out to achieve this. Although a number of distinguished architects were involved in the suburb's house designs, it was Lutyens alone who was responsible for planning Central Square, its churches, houses and public buildings. He began work on St Jude's in 1909 and on the Free Church in 1910 and even though the churches bear similarities in form they demonstrate differences too; certainly, their exteriors share a common style characterised by enormous pitch roofs and dormers, yet the Free Church has a low concrete dome (much in keeping with the Byzantine style) while St Jude's boasts a striking spire of grey and red brick, visible from miles around.

The interiors of the churches are quite dissimilar: while St Jude's is highly coloured, full of stained glass, paintings, murals and memorials (including one to horses killed in the First World War), the Free Church is simply decorated, its walls painted in pastel colours. Perhaps it is because of its plainer decoration and its enormous Tuscan columns that the Free Church appears the more spacious of the two and has an entirely different ambiance.

St Jude's Church. (Courtesy of A. McMurdo)

Free Church. (Courtesy of A. McMurdo)

Having excellent acoustics the churches are natural venues for concerts, which are held regularly throughout the year. A particular highlight for all local residents is the annual summer 'Proms at St Jude's Music and Literary Festival'.

www.stjudeonthehill.com
www.hgsfreechurch.org.uk

41. Witanhurst, No. 41 Highgate West Hill

Witanhurst, with over sixty-five rooms, claims to be the second-largest private house in London after Buckingham Palace. It is a striking palatial mansion, built between 1913 and 1920 for Sir Arthur Crosfield (1865–1938), the soap magnate and MP for Warrington (1906–10). Today the house is owned by Andrey Guryev, a Russian billionaire oligarch who over the past decade has been responsible for the addition

Witanhurst. (Courtesy of A. McMurdo)

Above: Witanhurst gatehouse. (Courtesy of A. McMurdo)

Left: Witanhust entrance gates. (Courtesy of A. McMurdo)

of an enormous two-storey underground basement providing staff accommodation, a cinema, parking for twenty-five cars as well as a swimming pool, sauna and gym. The main body of the house is built in the style of William and Mary, often described as 'Wrenaissance', and contains many lavishly decorated rooms such as the Chinese, music, billiard and dining rooms, as well as a ballroom and gallery.

Witanhurst is famous for its extensive grounds overlooking the City of London and Hampstead Heath and boasts a stunning listed Italianate garden, as well as a tennis pavilion. Every year Sir Arthur Crosfield and his Greek-born wife Domini held a tennis party here prior to or after the annual summer Wimbledon tennis tournament. This was a huge affair full of society and royal guests (attended by our present Queen when she was a princess) and naturally became a most important fixture in the society calendar of the time. Domini, who outlived her husband by twenty-five years, continued the parties and musical concerts until her own death in 1963. Ownership of Witanhurst subsequently passed to their adopted son Paul who sold it in 1970 to a property developer, after which it changed hands several times. Throughout the late 1900s plans were put forward to redevelop the house and grounds into perhaps a hotel or luxury housing, although nothing ever materialised. Between 2002 and 2004, despite its somewhat neglected appearance, Witanhurst was the location for the popular BBC show *Fame Academy*.

The entire estate was finally sold for £50 million in 2008 to its present owner. It would be interesting to know what Sir Arthur Crosfield would have made of Witanhurst's recent changes since it was he who led the successful campaign from 1918 to 1925 to preserve the Kenwood estate from development.

42. Holly Village and Holly Lodge Estate, Swain's Lane, Highgate

Towards the bottom of Swain's Lane and facing the railings of Highgate Cemetery (q.v.) is the most fantastically ornate Gothic group of houses known as Holly Village. Designed in 1865 by the architect Henry Astley Darbishire (1825–99), the village was built for the heiress and philanthropist Baroness Angela Burdett-Coutts (1814–1906), who owned a summer house, Holly Lodge, close by.

The village comprises twelve cottages encompassing a green and each building is covered with an interesting array of Gothic features such as turrets, spires, pointed arches, gargoyles and gables. The materials used in its construction are of the highest quality and the ornamentation is exceptional, especially the patterned

Above and previous page: Holly Village. (Courtesy of A. McMurdo)

brickwork and stone and woodcarvings – the work of Italian artisans. Miss Burdett-Coutts (who received the title of baroness in 1871) initially leased the cottages to those with sizeable incomes, for this was planned as model housing and not as one of her many charitable developments, but in the 1920s the situation changed and tenants were then able to purchase their homes. During the 1970s the singer-songwriter Lynsey de Paul (1948–2014) lived here and claimed her house was haunted. Certainly, on a misty winter's day it would be easy to believe that ghostly figures inhabit the village.

Angela Burdett-Coutts's fortune, which resulted in her becoming the second-wealthiest woman in the country after Queen Victoria, was bequeathed to her by the widow of her financier grandfather Thomas Coutts. Angela's lifelong generosity was legendary, and she gave support to numerous causes, especially those relating to women and children. In 1881 she broke the provisions of the will by marrying a foreigner, William Ashmead Bartlett (1851–1921), which led to her losing some 60 per cent of her wealth. Nonetheless, she and William (who was thirty-seven years her junior) seemed to enjoy a happy marriage and when she died in 1906, he inherited all her wealth and estate. Although he then tried to sell Holly Lodge it was only after William's death that it was sold and the land was developed into a gated garden suburb, the Holly Lodge estate, characterised by its large blocks of mock-Tudor mansion flats and hillsides filled with large suburban houses.

Above and right: Holly Lodge estate.
(Courtesy of A. McMurdo)

43. Cholmeley Lodge, Cholmeley Park, Highgate

Cholmeley Lodge is a fine example of art deco/streamline moderne architecture with its mix of curves and horizontal lines and immediately recognisable at the junction of Cholmeley Park and Highgate Hill. Designed by the architect Guy Morgan (1903–87), the building was originally supposed to grace Bournemouth's seafront. However, as its modern style failed to meet with the local council's approval Morgan moved his project to Highgate where, despite meeting local opposition, the plans were ultimately given the go ahead, and the building was completed in 1934.

Above and left: Cholmeley Lodge.
(Courtesy of A. McMurdo)

Taking the unusual form of three dramatically curved concave blocks, the Grade II listed flats are built in yellow brick and light stone and arranged over six floors. There are four entrance doorways under curved canopies and the name 'Cholmeley Lodge' is inscribed above each in elegant art deco white lettering.

The flats are built on the site of the former mansion Cholmeley Lodge, which was demolished in 1931 and takes its name from Roger Cholmeley, who established Highgate School (q.v.) in 1565. Guy Morgan completed the building before embarking on Florin Court in Charterhouse Square (the detective's home in the ITV series of *Poirot*), and it is believed to be his inspiration for it.

44. Isokon Flats, Lawn Road, Hampstead

The brainchild of Canadian architect Wells Coates, the Isokon flats were built for Jack and Molly Pritchard in 1933–34. Originally there were thirty-two minimalist flats, a mere 24 square metres in size, and designed to be cheap dwellings for single professional people. All had fitted space-saving furniture and the majority were built as studio flats – the single room being divided into living and sleeping areas either by bookcases or a semi-open screen. The Pritchards lived in a one-bed penthouse on the roof with their children occupying the studio penthouse next door. Furnishings were mainly supplied through Jack and Molly's company – Isokon Laminated Furniture – and built to the designs of Marcel Breuer, an architect and former master at the Bauhaus, whom Pritchard had helped in his flight to the UK from fascist Europe in the 1930s.

When the block was completed residents had use of a communal ground-floor kitchen, but Marcel Breuer and FRS Yorke converted it in 1936–37 into a residents' club, the Isobar. The club rapidly became an elite social meeting place for Isokon's residents, particularly its many artists, intellectuals and refugees, and also for others in their circle who lived nearby. Bauhaus masters Walter Gropius and Laszlo Moholy-Nagy, the author Agatha Christie and artists such as Ben

Isokon flats. (Courtesy of A. McMurdo)

Nicholson, Barbara Hepworth and Henry Moore all mingled here in the 1930s and 1940s.

In 2003, following a period of neglect, the building was thoroughly refurbished, after which time some of the units were sold on leases but the majority were offered to key workers on a shared-ownership basis. An exhibition gallery was opened downstairs, and this is where visitors now come to learn about Isokon's architectural and social history and the residents who once lived here. Run by volunteers, the gallery is open on weekends from March until October.

Isokon today is a Grade I listed building both for its architectural design and in recognition of it being the first of such modernist apartment blocks in the country. The flats are considered to be a great expression of 1930s communal and minimal living and many of them still retain their original furnishings and interiors.

www.isokongallery.org

45. Highpoint I and II, North Hill, Highgate

These two white towers are a wonderful testament to the work of the Russian émigré architect Berthold Lubetkin (1901–90) and his architectural practice Tecton. The flats erected in two phases (1933–35 and 1936–38) are a truly outstanding example of the International modern style of architecture and have received enormous praise in the years since they were built. Le Corbusier, regarded as the pioneer of the Modern Movement, described Highpoint I as 'an achievement of the highest rank' following his visit in 1935 and architectural historian Dan Cruickshank was so impressed by Lubetkin's work that he included it as one of only eight sites in his book *Britain's Best Buildings*.

Although Lubetkin's commission had been to design the apartments as housing for factory workers, the idea was later abandoned and instead Highpoint was built to accommodate a wide range of residents. However, from the start the flats, with their extensive grounds, swimming pool and tennis courts appealed to a middle-class clientele and, like the nearby Isokon flats (q.v.), became attractive to European refugees too.

Highpoint I and II are adjacent to one another on the top of North Hill set back from the road behind large mature trees. They exhibit many features of the International Style: long, narrow windows, a rectilinear form with little colour or decoration and built of reinforced concrete, looking much like white concrete boxes. Highpoint II, on its completion in 1938, was criticised by young architects of the day as they considered that Lubetkin had demonstrated signs of a move away from the pure modernist style. Look carefully and you will see it not only has a patterned façade, but the main entrance porch is partially supported by two caryatids – ornamentation much more in keeping with classical rather than modernist buildings of the period. (It is said that Lubetkin placed the sculptures here to placate the local residents, who opposed his stark style of architecture alongside the surrounding Georgian and Victorian housing.)

Lubetkin initially occupied Highpoint II's penthouse flat, which subsequently became known as the 'Georgian Dacha' on account of its interior furnishings, rough pine timber panelling and its curved ceiling.

Right: High Point 1 entrance. (Courtesy of A. McMurdo)

Below: High Point 1 and 2. (Courtesy of A. McMurdo)

46. No. 2 Willow Road, Hampstead

Completed in the late 1930s, the row of modernist terraced houses at Nos 1–3
Willow Road was designed by the Marxist Hungarian-born architect and furniture
designer Erno Goldfinger (1902–87) to replace a former terrace dating to the
1700s. Goldfinger's plans for his project caused great controversy, which led to a
loud and sustained campaign against him by local residents under the leadership
of Lord Brooke of Cumnor, later the MP for Hampstead. One of their number,
a certain Ian Fleming and creator of the *James Bond* books, was said to be so
incensed by the proposed development that he appropriated the architect's name
for his chief villain when writing *Goldfinger*, with the upshot that the two men
almost proceeded to litigation. Despite this opposition Goldfinger maintained his
proposed houses to be 'an adaptation of the eighteenth-century style' and claimed
they displayed all the classical divisions of basement, piano nobile and attic so
were in keeping with the period houses in nearby Downshire Hill. Goldfinger's
modernism was radical, which explains why the terrace is built in concrete and
faced in red brick and not the more common 'white box' design associated with
other modernist architects such as Le Corbusier, Lubetkin or Coates.

No. 2 Willow Road was built by Erno Goldfinger as his family home, and he
designed much of its interior. Today it is owned by the National Trust and open

No. 2 Willow Road. (Courtesy of A. McMurdo)

to visitors who marvel at Goldfinger's imaginative and inventive furniture, some free-standing, some fitted. A tour around the house allows one to see Goldfinger's personal possessions, understand more about his way of life and to view his art collection, which contains works by Henry Moore, Max Ernst, Man Ray and Barbara Hepworth – all artists he and his wife, Ursula, socialised with. The Goldfingers were an intrinsic part of Hampstead's intellectual set, frequently mixing with its many writers and idealist thinkers.

In the post-war years Goldfinger progressed his style into brutalism and although his design of Trellick Tower, a high-rise apartment block in West London, was initially reviled it is now considered an excellent example of brutalist architecture and bears Grade II* status.

www.nationaltrust.org.uk

47. Royal Free Hospital, Pond Street, Hampstead

Founded almost 200 years ago the Royal Free Hospital was established by the surgeon William Marsden as a hospital for those unable to afford healthcare. Marsden's inspiration for setting it up had come from his experience of finding a young girl dying of consumption (TB) on the steps of a church in Holborn. He tried to get medical help for her in several of the city's voluntary hospitals but with no money and no letters of recommendation she was turned away and died at Marsden's own lodgings a few

Below and overleaf: Royal Free Hospital. (Courtesy of A. McMurdo)

days later. Determined to change matters he proposed a free hospital to be funded by donation and public subscription, stating that 'the only passport should be poverty and disease'. The hospital opened in 1828 and was first called the London General Institution for the Gratuitous Care of Malignant Diseases but was later renamed the London Free Hospital. Queen Victoria, on ascending the throne in 1837, awarded it a royal charter and since then its official title has been the Royal Free Hospital.

In 1842 the hospital moved into former barracks on the Gray's Inn Road where it provided free treatment to everyone. In 1877 it became a teaching hospital and was the only London hospital to accept female medical students until 1947. Over the years the hospital expanded greatly, establishing new departments, including among others maternity, gynaecology, obstetrics, outpatients and casualty. When the National Health Service was established in 1948 the Royal Free Hospital united with several smaller hospitals to form the Royal Free Group. Having outgrown its site, the hospital finally relocated to its present purpose-built premises in Pond Street in 1974. Since 2012 it has operated as the Royal Free London NHS Foundation Trust, which nowadays incorporates Barnet and Chase Farm hospitals as well.

The Royal Free has always had a reputation for its innovative groundbreaking research and a new centre, the UCL Institute of Immunity and Transplantation (IIT) Pears Building, opened alongside the main hospital in 2021. Here scientists, medical staff and patients will be brought together in clinical trials to help develop radical new treatments for diseases such as leukaemia and diabetes.

www.royalfree.nhs.org

48. Nos 6, 6.5 and 27a Redington Road, Hampstead

Until the mid-nineteenth century Redington Road was undeveloped, an area of fields and streams, the latter tributaries of the River Westbourne. The land was owned by the Maryon Wilson family who gradually sold off small plots of their estate to ensure that the appearance of the area remained largely unspoilt. No. 6, one of the earliest houses developed here in 1876 as the vicarage for St John-at-Hampstead Church, was built in the Gothic style with a pointed turret, large chimneys and high-pitched roof. In 2007 a contemporary house, No. 6.5, The Cottage, was built alongside it in a wholly different style that is dominated by its stunning floor-to-ceiling glazed façade. At the time of writing, this property was on the market for a price of £7 million.

A short distance away No. 27a Redington Road has a most distinctive appearance. Constructed in 2005, this narrow house sits wedged between substantial period properties and has its main entrance in Chesterford Gardens. The house, identified by its green copper barrel roof and porthole window, is made from certified sustainable timber, uses solar power to heat water and is insulated with sheep's wool. An excellent view of its interior spiral staircase is obtained through the large ground-to-roof front window.

Above: Nos 6 and 6.5 Redington Road. (Courtesy of A. McMurdo)

Left: No. 27a Redington Road. (Courtesy of A. McMurdo)

49. Nos 81 and 85 Swain's Lane, Highgate

Nos 81 and 85 Swain's Lane are found on either side of Highgate West Cemetery's gatehouse. John Winter's 'Modern House' (No. 81) is located immediately to the left of it, while Eldridge Smerin's house (No. 85) is on the right, a little further up the hill. Despite being built forty years apart, the properties share common features, the most obvious of which are their rectilinear shape and substantial use of glass, ensuring interiors are flooded with natural light.

John Winter designed No. 81 in 1967 as a private house for his own use. Built on a small plot it has an internal steel frame as well as external COR-TEN steel cladding, the latter considered revolutionary at the time in domestic construction as it is a weathering carbon steel that rusts. However, No. 81 has since become one of the most influential modern steel houses in the country.

No. 85, arranged over four floors, has stunning views over the cemetery through its frameless rear glass walls, and has a large retractable glass roof that transforms the top floor into a splendid open courtyard. The house may appear familiar as it has been used as a filming venue in the TV series *Spooks*, *Waking the Dead* and *Luther*.

No. 81 Swain's Lane. (Courtesy of A. McMurdo)

No. 85 Swain's Lane. (Courtesy of A. McMurdo)

50. Channing School and the Arundel Centre, The Bank, Highgate

The Arundel Centre opened as Channing School's new Performing Arts Centre in 2018. Immediately acclaimed for its facilities and architecture, it was placed on RIBA's shortlist of the 'Best New Buildings in London 2019'. The building, designed by Buckley Gray Yeoman Architects (BGY), faces Highgate Hill and is easily identified by its use of warm red brick, high-pitched roof, canopy, and glazed entrance lobby. BGY has cleverly aligned the new building with the historic Founders Hall nearby and has taken great care to ensure it fits in with the other

Arundel Centre, Channing Senior School. (Courtesy of A. McMurdo)

Fairseat House, Channing Junior School. (Courtesy of A. McMurdo)

school campus buildings. The state-of-the-art centre has been equipped with professional lighting, rigging and sound facilities, allowing the students to learn technical theatre production skills as well as providing a truly flexible space for drama and performance. Moreover, the architects' design has allowed the Arundel Centre to be used as much for rehearsal as for major school productions.

When the school was first established in the late nineteenth century it occupied just one building beside Cholmeley Park. It has since grown extensively and now stretches along much of The Bank, including, among other buildings, two listed Grade II Regency townhouses at Nos 120 and 122. Channing School was founded in 1885 by Unitarians to educate their daughters and was named after an American minister, W. E. Channing, who had visited the UK in 1822 to meet up with Coleridge. It is still the only Unitarian school in the country and retains its founding principles of tolerance and kindness. While The Bank is home to the senior school, the junior school is located on Highgate High Street beside Waterlow Park in Fairseat House. Fairseat sits on the site of Sir Roger Cholmeley's (q.v. Highgate School) former home and in 1856 a lease was taken out on it by Alderman Sydney Waterlow (1822–1906), later Lord Mayor of London. Despite being exceedingly wealthy, Waterlow was never able to buy the freehold of the property, but he did rename it Fairseat, using the title of his father-in-law's house in Kent. He had the house rebuilt in 1867 in the French Renaissance style characterised in particular by its steep, tiled mansard roof.

Acknowledgements

The author would like to thank all the many people that have helped in the production of this book and to pay particular tribute to the role of her husband and photographer, Alex McMurdo, whose beautiful images adorn its pages bringing the buildings to life. Both he and Jo also deserve thanks for their great support, taking the time to proofread the text and give critical feedback. I am also extremely grateful for help and assistance given to me by Hampstead Parish Church and by Dr Ian Dungavell at the Friends of Highgate Cemetery Trust.

Furthermore, the author would like to thank Amberley Publishing for commissioning this book and to acknowledge the excellent support and hard work of Jenny Bennett, Becky Cadenhead and the whole production team.

About the Author

Lucy McMurdo is a modern history graduate and native Londoner who has lived in the capital all her life. In 2003 when she qualified as a London Blue Badge Tourist Guide she combined two of her major loves – history and London – and has been sharing her knowledge of the city with local and foreign visitors ever since. Always keen to explore and learn about London's secrets, she spends many hours 'walking the streets' looking out for hidden corners, unusual curiosities as well as architecturally significant buildings and ones that have a story to tell.

Lucy's tour-guiding career began over thirty years ago when she first guided overseas visitors around the UK. Since then, in addition to tour guiding she has been greatly involved in training and examining the next generation of tour guides. She has created, taught and run courses in London's University of Westminster and City University, and also developed guide training programmes for the warders and site guides at Hampton Court Palace.

Most recently Lucy has been writing about the city she is so passionate about and is the author of six London guidebooks: *Islington & Clerkenwell in 50 Buildings*, *Chiswick in 50 Buildings*, *Bloomsbury in 50 Buildings*, *Explore London's Square Mile*, *Streets of London* and *London in 7 Days*.